Heroes and Villains

MARTIN LUTHER KING JR.

Other books in the Heroes and Villains series include:

Heroes and Villains

MARTIN LUTHER KING JR.

Michael V. Uschan

Antioch Community High School
Library

**LUCENT
BOOKS®**

THOMSON
GALE

San Diego • Detroit • New York • San Francisco • Cleveland • New Haven, Conn. • Waterville, Maine • London • Munich

To Ray W. Doherty, who fought for racial equality through his church.

© 2004 by Lucent Books. Lucent Books is an imprint of The Gale Group, Inc., a division of Thomson Learning, Inc.

Lucent Books® and Thomson Learning™ are trademarks used herein under license.

For more information, contact
Lucent Books
27500 Drake Rd.
Farmington Hills, MI 48331-3535
Or you can visit our Internet site at http://www.gale.com

LIBRARY OF CONGRESS CATALOGING-IN-PUBLICATION DATA

Uschan, Michael V., 1948–
    Martin Luther King, Jr. / by Michael V. Uschan.
        p . cm. — (Heroes and villains)
Summary: Profiles the Baptist minister who led the nonviolent struggle for African Americans' civil rights during the 1960s.
Includes bibliographical references and index.
    ISBN 1-59018-257-X (hardcover : alk. paper)
    1. King, Martin Luther, Jr. 1929–1968.—Juvenile literature. 2. African Americans—Biography—Juvenile literature 3. Civil Rights workers—United States—Biography—Juvenile literature. 4. Baptists—United States—Clergy—Biography—Juvenile literature. 5. Afican Americans—Civil rights—History—20th Century—Juvenile literature [1. King, Martin Luther, Jr. , 1929–1968 2. Civil rights workers. 3. Clergy. 4. Civil rights movements—History. 5. African Americans—Biography] I. Title. II. Heroes and villains series.
    E185.97 K5U83 2004
    323'. 092—dc22
                                                                        2003011686

Printed in the United States of America

Contents

Good and evil are an ever-present feature of human history. Their presence is reflected through the ages in tales of great heroism and extraordinary villainy. Such tales provide insight into human nature, whether they involve two people or two thousand, for the essence of heroism and villainy is found in deeds rather than in numbers. It is the deeds that pique our interest and lead us to wonder what prompts a man or woman to perform such acts.

Samuel Johnson, the eminent eighteenth-century English writer, once wrote, "The two great movers of the human mind are the desire for good, and fear of evil." The pairing of desire and fear, possibly two of the strongest human emotions, helps explain the intense fascination people have with all things good and evil—and by extension, heroic and villainous.

People are attracted to the person who reaches into a raging river to pull a child from what could have been a watery grave for both, and to the person who risks his or her own life to shepherd hundreds of desperate black slaves to safety on the Underground Railroad. We wonder what qualities these heroes possess that enable them to act against self-interest, and even their own survival. We also wonder if, under similar circumstances, we would behave as they do.

Evil, on the other hand, horrifies as well as intrigues us. Few people can look upon the drifter who mutilates and kills a neighbor or the dictator who presides over the torture and murder of thousands of his own citizens without feeling a sense of revulsion. And yet, as Joseph Conrad writes, we experience "the fascination of the abomination." How else to explain the overwhelming success of a book such as Truman Capote's *In Cold Blood*, which examines in horrifying detail a vicious and senseless murder that took place in the American heartland in the 1960s? The popularity of murder mysteries and Court TV are also evidence of the human fascination with villainy.

Most people recoil in the face of such evil. Yet most feel a deep-seated curiosity about the kind of person who could commit a terrible act. It is perhaps a reflection of our innermost fears that we wonder whether we could resist or stand up to such behavior in our presence or even if we ourselves possess the capacity to commit such terrible crimes.

The Lucent Books Heroes and Villains series capitalizes on our fascination with the perpetrators of both good and evil by introducing readers to some of history's most revered heroes and hated villains. These include heroes such as Frederick Douglass, who knew firsthand the humiliation of slavery and, at great risk to himself, publicly fought to abolish the institution of slavery in America. It also includes villains such as Adolf Hitler, who is remembered both for the devastation of Europe and for the murder of 6 million Jews and thousands of Gypsies, Slavs, and others whom Hitler deemed unworthy of life.

Each book in the Heroes and Villains series examines the life story of a hero or villain from history. Generous use of primary and secondary source quotations gives readers eyewitness views of the life and times of each individual as well as enlivens the narrative. Notes and annotated bibliographies provide stepping-stones to further research.

A Disciple of Nonviolence

There are two theories about why some people become great leaders. One explanation is that the pressure of historical events, such as war or great social change, forces people to become great to meet challenges confronting them. But President Harry S. Truman, who in 1945 irrevocably changed history by making the difficult decision to drop the atomic bomb on Japan to end World War II, was a firm believer in the second theory—that leaders shape historical events because they have the capacity to be great. "Men make history," claimed Truman. "History does not make the man."[1]

In his biography of Martin Luther King Jr., Lerone Bennett Jr. claims King was a great leader because he was able to shape the events of his time. In *What Manner of Man: A Biography of Martin Luther King, Jr.*, Bennett wrote that King did this by igniting a fight for civil rights that continues today:

[There] is a sharp distinction between the leader who transcends events he did not create and the truly great leader who transcends events, men, and perhaps even time by creating not only his greatness but also the occasion of his greatness. No leader, of course, can create an event the time is not prepared for. But the genius of the great leader lies precisely in his apprehension of what the times require and in carrying through in the teeth of great opposition an act that changes the times. King approached that kind of greatness, creating the occasion of the "Negro Revolution."[2]

Martin Luther King Jr. rides a bus in Montgomery, Alabama. King's participation in the 1955 bus boycott in Montgomery propelled him to the forefront of the Civil Rights movement.

King did not create the Civil Rights movement by himself. But as Bennett notes, King's greatness was that he was able to perceive what his era was demanding—racial justice for blacks. King also showed his greatness by daring to challenge racism where it was the strongest and most virulent, in the South in which he lived.

A Powerful Weapon

The cities of Montgomery and Birmingham in Alabama were the scenes of King's most famous battles to secure for blacks the basic civil liberties that white U.S. citizens had always taken for granted but which blacks had always been denied. It was in Montgomery in 1956 that this unknown young Baptist minister first became known to the nation and the world by leading a drive to give blacks the right to do a very simple thing—ride a bus without fear of discrimination. In 1963 King challenged racism in Birmingham, where peaceful marchers demanding an end

9

to segregation in restaurants and other public places were greeted by club-wielding policemen and attack dogs.

In the very different fights he waged in both cities, King's most powerful weapon was his doctrine of nonviolence. King would cling tightly to this philosophy despite explosives hurled at his Montgomery home and the mindless brutality in Birmingham—a city that would become known as "Bombingham" because racists bombed churches and homes to kill innocent blacks. In Birmingham, King explained how nonviolence could triumph over violence:

> We will meet the forces of hate with the power of love. We must say to our white brothers all over the South, We will match your capacity to inflict suffering with our capacity to endure suffering. Bomb our homes and we will still love you. We will so appeal to your heart and conscience that we will win you in the process.[3]

The Power of Nonviolence

The essence of King's philosophy can be found in one of the most well-known commands of Jesus Christ—that people should turn the other cheek if someone slaps them. In Montgomery, King brought that biblical injunction to life with peaceful protests that defeated the hatred and physical violence with which they were countered.

The arrest of Rosa Parks on December 1, 1955, for refusing to give up her seat to a white man on a segregated bus is often cited as the starting point of the Civil Rights movement. King, pastor of a local church, was named to lead an effort that within a year would result in integration of Montgomery buses.

The tactics King adopted in Montgomery were peaceful. Blacks refused to ride buses, which financially crippled the city-run system because most of its customers were black. King also decided not to retaliate against violent incidents by racist whites who opposed them. Montgomery thus set the standard for scores of similar black protests in the coming years—all would begin peacefully and remain that way even when racist whites reacted with violence.

The Power of a Dream

Another reason King was able to win civil rights battles was his ability to inspire people with the cause for which he fought. King biographer Louis E. Lomax wrote that while King was still alive, "In some instinctive way, he helps Negroes understand how they themselves feel and why they feel as they do."[4]

King also had the ability to communicate to whites, in simple human terms they could understand, how racism affected blacks. For the first time King made many white people aware of the suffering and injustice that blacks were forced to live with on a daily basis.

King's message was all the more dramatic because of the eloquence of his words.

King wielded his power with words never more strongly than on August 28, 1963, when he gave his famous "I Have A Dream" speech on the steps of the Lincoln Memorial. In an inspired talk to an estimated 250,000 people gathered for the March on Washington, D.C., King dared to dream of a future

Nearly 250,000 people gather for the 1963 March on Washington, D.C. Martin Luther King delivered his famous "I Have a Dream" speech at this rally.

in which people of all races and religions could live together in loving harmony. King said he longed to see

> [T]hat day when all of God's children, black men and white men, Jews and Gentiles, Protestants and Catholics, will be able to join hands and sing in the words of the old Negro spiritual, "Free at last! free at last! thank God Almighty, we are free at last!"[5]

Not Just King

Although King came to be considered one of the great figures in U.S. history, he always understood he was only a small part of the Civil Rights movement. King stressed this in the introduction to *Stride Toward Freedom*, his book about the Montgomery bus boycott:

> While the nature of this account causes me to make frequent use of the pronoun "I," in every important part of the story it should be "we." This is not a drama with only one actor [but] the chronicle of 50,000 Negroes who took to heart the principles of nonviolence, who learned to fight for their rights with the weapon of love.[6]

However, his book is also the story of the man who led them, a leader who was able to make history as well as write about it.

Chapter One

A Preacher's Son

In 1939 Atlanta, Georgia, hosted the premiere of *Gone With The Wind*, an epic movie about the Civil War and its grim aftermath in the South that is considered one of the greatest films ever made. Atlanta was chosen because it was the home of Margaret Mitchell, who wrote the book of the same title. It was also home to ten-year-old Martin Luther King Jr.

The hundreds of Atlanta residents chosen to participate in the festivities were excited because they could mingle with movie stars like Clark Gable and Vivien Leigh and because reporters and photographers from around the nation recorded the event. One of the lucky locals who won a role was Martin, who appeared in a choir that sang songs in front of a replica of Tara, a mansion in the movie.

Martin and the other choir members in the pre–Civil War scene represented more than singers—they were playing the roles of slaves. Although King biographer Michael Eric Dyson writes that "the thought of King appearing as a 'happy darky' is jarring," Dyson admits there was great irony in the fact that the future civil rights leader "took his first bow on the national stage in a setting that was symptomatic of the cruel southern racial politics he would help to change fifteen years later."[7]

The movie was filled with racist stereotypes—that blacks were lazy, stupid, and untrustworthy and that they had actually been better off before the Civil War freed them. But in the Atlanta of 1939 such views, no matter how repugnant they are today, were accepted by whites. Although as an

Martin Luther King Jr. was born in this Atlanta, Georgia, house on January 15, 1929.

adult King would lead the battle to free blacks of the stigma of such false beliefs and the racist treatment they fostered, while growing up, young Martin had to endure them.

King's Family

When Martin was born on January 15, 1929, he was christened Michael Luther King Jr., but in 1933 his father changed both of their first names to Martin. King Sr. did this after the death of his own father, James Albert King, who had always claimed he named his son "Martin" and "Luther" after two of his brothers, only to have it recorded incorrectly on the birth certificate. On his deathbed James asked his son to correct the mistake.

When Martin was born, his father was pastor of Atlanta's Ebeneezer Baptist Church; his mother, Alberta, was the daughter of the Reverend A.D. Williams, who had headed Ebeneezer until he died in 1931. The couple married on Thanksgiving Day 1926 and would have three children—Christine, Martin, and Alfred Daniel, who, like his maternal grandfather, became known by the initials A.D.

Martin's father was born into poverty on a farm in rural Stockbridge, Georgia. When he was sixteen, he left home for Atlanta, where he worked hard to better himself. "I may *smell* like a mule, but I don't *think* like a mule,"[8] was the rural youth's proud boast. The poorly educated but highly motivated

King Sr. took night classes and became pastor of two small, rural churches.

After he married, King Sr. began attending Morehouse College, a school for blacks in Atlanta, and received a bachelor's degree in divinity. His father-in-law, an important civic leader, had helped found the city's first chapter of the National Association for the Advancement of Colored People (NAACP), the national organization of blacks and whites that fought for civil rights. When King Sr. became Ebeneezer's pastor, he assumed Williams's high-profile position in the community.

Martin's Youth

Although Martin grew up during the Great Depression, the worst economic crisis in the nation's history, he had a comfortable life. The Kings lived in a nice brick home and were better off financially than most people, white or black. His father, nicknamed "Daddy King," liked to claim, "We've never lived in a rented house and never ridden too long in a car on which payment was due."[9]

Martin was smart and began attending school at the age of five, a year earlier than the law allowed. But when Martin boasted about his fifth birthday party at school, he was expelled until the following year. When Martin was allowed back after turning six, he became a good student.

In addition to what Martin learned at school, his father taught him valuable lessons about life, including the importance of working for what he wanted. King Sr. made Martin take jobs to make money to buy toys like a baseball or a kite. When Martin was eight, he began delivering a black daily newspaper to homes of subscribers, and when he was eleven, he started delivering the *Atlanta Journal*, a white newspaper. As a teenager, Martin spent a lot of money on clothes, and his friends nicknamed him "Tweed" because he always dressed stylishly. Martin also enjoyed many sports during his youth. He swam, played tennis, and wrestled, and he was a key player on neighborhood baseball and football teams.

But even though his father was comfortable financially and respected by blacks and even many whites, Martin's childhood was not free from the racism that tainted the lives of every southern black. To whites Martin would always be black—and that meant he was inferior.

A Segregated Youth

For Martin growing up in Atlanta meant living under the dismal spell of Jim Crow, the nickname for the racist laws that segregated southern blacks and denied them many of their basic rights and liberties. White southerners created Jim Crow in the decades after the Civil War to keep blacks in an inferior position.

Jim Crow laws mandated that blacks and whites attend separate schools, ride in different areas on buses and trains, and use separate public facilities such as restrooms and drinking fountains, which were always clearly labeled "white" or "colored." "WHITES ONLY" signs were displayed at restaurants, hotels, movie theaters, golf courses, and other establishments that barred blacks.

Martin was insulated from some of the insulting effects of Jim Crow. For example blacks who rode the bus had to enter through the front door, pay their fare, and then back out and re-enter through the rear door. When they got on the bus again, they could sit only in the back. Because his father had a car, Martin and his siblings rarely had to endure this degrading experience, which they hated.

Lessons in Racism

But every black growing up in the South eventually had to learn to deal with racism, and Martin's first experience was a bitter one. Despite segregation, southerners allowed young children of both races to be playmates, and young Martin had two white friends. But when they began attending segregated schools, the white boys' mother decided her sons could no longer be friends with blacks; she told them to stay away from Martin. For the first time Martin learned how the color of his skin could affect his life.

When Martin was eight, his father took him to buy a new pair of shoes. A

Men in the South use separate drinking fountains. Segregated drinking fountains, restrooms, and other public facilities were the norm during King's youth.

store clerk refused to help them until they moved to seats in the rear. "We'll either buy shoes sitting here or we won't buy any shoes at all,"[10] his father said. When the clerk would not relent, the Kings walked out. And once in a downtown store when Martin was eleven a white woman shrieked, "The little nigger stepped on my foot."[11] She then slapped him. In the South whites—even young children and women—could hit blacks without fear of any consequences.

King was a proud person even as a child, and such racial slights angered him. The most humiliating experience of his youth happened when he was in the eleventh grade and he rode to another town with his favorite teacher to enter a speaking contest held by the Negro

Elks. On the trip home, after winning with a speech titled "The Negro and the Constitution," Martin and his teacher were forced to give up their seats to white passengers. Claiming it was "the angriest I have ever been in my life," King admitted years later he hated being treated that way:

> I could never adjust to the separate waiting rooms, separate eating places, separate restrooms, partly because the separate [facility] was always unequal and partly because the very idea of separate did something to my sense of dignity and self respect.[12]

Morehouse College

One reason King hated being considered inferior is that he knew he was smarter and better educated than many whites who treated him that way. Although Daddy King had never gone to school for more than three months in any single year until he was fifteen, he tried to give his children the best education possible. Martin went to Yonge Street Elementary School, the Atlanta University Laboratory School, and Booker T. Washington High School, which were among the finest in Atlanta for blacks.

King passed the entrance examination to Atlanta's Morehouse College while still a high school junior, which allowed him to enroll in college with-

out graduating. He was only fifteen in September 1944 when he began taking classes at Morehouse. King, however, soon realized the education he had received in segregated schools had been inferior; he could only read at the eighth grade level and had trouble writing coherent sentences.

In the next few years King worked hard to overcome his academic weaknesses, learning from teachers like Professor Gladstone Lewis Chandler, who encouraged him to build his vocabulary and improve his English. At Morehouse, King began to acquire the words and grammatical skills that would help him become a spellbinding speaker and an eloquent writer.

King also participated in many activities. He played football, sang in the glee club, and helped establish the college's youth chapter of the NAACP. His membership in the Intercollegiate Council, which included black and white students from area colleges, taught him one of the most important lessons of his life. While admitting that the racial indignities of his youth had started to make him bitter toward whites, King said his attitude changed as he began to know more white people:

> The wholesome relations we had in this group convinced me that we [blacks] have many white persons as allies, particularly among the younger generation. I had been ready to resent the whole white race, but as

Jim Crow Segregation

The body of legislation that restricted the rights of African Americans in the twentieth century was known collectively as "Jim Crow." The laws were named after a character in an early nineteenth-century minstrel show who blackened his face so he could perform as, and thus mock, blacks. This historical explanation of Jim Crow laws by Ronald L.F. Davis of California State University–Northridge is from the Jim Crow History Internet (www.jimcrowhistory.org):

The term Jim Crow originated in a song performed by Daddy Rice, a white minstrel show entertainer in the 1830s. Rice covered his face with charcoal paste or burnt cork to resemble a black man, and then sang and danced a routine in caricature of a silly black person. By the 1850s, this Jim Crow character, one of several stereotypical images of black inferiority in the nation's popular culture, was a standard act in the minstrel shows of the day. How it became a term synonymous with the brutal segregation and disfranchisement of African Americans in the late nineteenth-century is unclear. What is clear, however, is that by 1900, the term was generally identified with those racist laws and actions that deprived African-Americans of their civil rights by defining blacks as inferior to whites, as members of a caste of subordinate people. Blacks [in the early 20th Century] were required to sit in a special car reserved for blacks known as "The Jim Crow car," even if they had bought first-class tickets. Some states also passed laws banning interracial marriages. These bans were, in the opinion of some historians, the "ultimate segregation laws." They clearly announced that blacks were so inferior to whites that any mixing of the two threatened the very survival of the superior white race.

I got to see more white people my resentment was softened and a spirit of cooperation took its place.[13]

King learned more about racial tolerance during the summer of 1944 when he worked on a Connecticut tobacco farm to earn money. He discovered it was easier to be black in the North. King could dine at restaurants or watch movies in establishments that also served whites, and he did not have to worry constantly that he would do something that might accidentally offend a white person.

King reveled in that freedom. But when he traveled home by train at the end of the summer, Jim Crow once again dominated his life. King always remembered the despair he felt on that trip when he went to a dining car after the train had traveled back into the South. The waiter led him to a rear table and pulled a curtain down to hide his presence from white passengers, who the waiter thought might be uncomfortable that a black was in their midst. "I felt as though the curtain had dropped on my selfhood," King said.[14]

Choosing a Career

Like many college students King struggled to choose a career. At various times he considered studying to be a doctor or lawyer, but in his senior year King decided to become a Baptist minister. Even though he would be following in the footsteps of his father and grandfather, it was a difficult choice for King. He had always feared that being a pastor would restrict the kind of things he could accomplish in his life, especially his growing urge to fight racism.

But King began to realize that being a Baptist minister would not stop him from doing "something that transcends our immediate lives." He also began to see that his sermons, instead of mindless retellings of Bible stories or dramatic, shouted commands to church members to be good or risk damnation, could be "a respectable force for ideas, even social protest."[15]

On June 8, 1948, the nineteen-year-old King graduated from Morehouse with a bachelor's degree in sociology. He then attended Crozer Theological Seminary in Chester, Pennsylvania, to become a minister.

Crozer Seminary

At Crozer, King went to school for the first time with whites, who made up two-thirds of the student body. Fearing that he might do something to reinforce negative stereotypes that he believed whites had about blacks, King always conducted himself mindfully. He dressed and groomed himself with great care, was on time for every class, and always tried to act in a dignified manner. "I'm afraid I was grimly serious for a time,"[16] King admitted years later. But King need not have worried. He flourished academically at Crozer, where he received straight-A grades for three years, and became class valedictorian.

In addition to his theological studies, King devoured books by a wide variety of political theorists and philosophers. Said King, "Not until I entered Crozer Theological Seminary in 1948, however, did I begin a serious intellectual quest for a method to eliminate social evil."[17] King took bits and pieces from many great thinkers to formulate his own view of the world, one which led him to adopt the concept of nonviolence that would become the heart of the Civil Rights movement he would lead.

Coming to Believe in Nonviolence

At Morehouse, King was introduced to the idea of using passive resistance to attack social wrongs when he read "Civil Disobedience" by David Henry Thoreau. In this classic essay, the great

Two large trees stand in front of a dormitory at Crozer Theological Seminary. Martin Luther King began his studies at the school in 1948.

American philosopher explains why he was willing to go to jail in 1846 rather than pay a local tax; he did it as a personal protest against the Mexican War, which he believed was unjust.

At Crozer, King also began absorbing the philosophy of a world-famous political leader who had used nonviolent tactics to fight social wrongs—Mohandas Gandhi of India. King was so excited after attending a lecture on Gandhi's life that he immediately bought a half-dozen books about him. King read how Gandhi, who had also been influenced by Thoreau, conducted a campaign of peaceful resistance for nearly two decades to win his country's freedom from Great Britain, which had ruled India for over a century through military force.

Gandhi did this by fasting, conducting mass marches and other peaceful

Gandhi's Vision of Nonviolence

One of the great intellectual influences on Martin Luther King Jr. was Mohandas Gandhi of India, who used nonviolent protests to force Great Britain to grant his country its independence in 1947. In the King biography What Manner of Man, *author Lerone Bennett Jr. explains that King adopted the philosophy Gandhi had developed regarding nonviolent tactics as the foundation of the civil rights protests that King led. Bennett writes,*

Gandhi's campaign, which began long before King was born, covered a thirty-year span. During this period Gandhi employed a variety of techniques, fasts, general strikes, boycotts, mass marches, and massive civil disobedience. The key to his vision of battle, however, was nonresistance or *Satyagraha* which has been translated as soul force, the power of truth. *Satyagraha*, Gandhi wrote, "is the vindication of truth not by infliction of suffering on the opponent but on one's self." Throughout the long contest with Britain, Gandhi urged his followers to forswear violence and to work for ultimate reconciliation with their opponents by returning good for evil and by openly breaking unjust laws and willingly paying the penalty. "Rivers of blood," he said in a quote King would later

repeat, almost word for word, "may have to flow before we gain our freedom, but it must be our blood." Suffering and self-sacrifice were at the heart of Gandhi's philosophy. "The government of the day," he said, "has passed a law which is applicable to me. I do not like it. If by using violence I force the government to repeal the law, I am employing what may be called body-force. If I do not obey the law and accept the penalty for the breach [of law], I use soul-force. It involves sacrifice of self."

Indian activist Mohandas Gandhi proved to be a tremendous influence on Martin Luther King.

protests, and boycotting British goods, which hurt that country's economy. Those activities helped turn public opinion against English domination of his country, and in 1947 the British granted India its independence. The power of Gandhi's accomplishment helped King overcome his own doubts about whether nonviolence was a strong enough tactic to defeat a social evil like racism. Said King,

> My skepticism concerning the power of love gradually diminished, and I came to see for the first time its potency in the area of social reform. I came to feel that this was the only morally and practically sound method open to oppressed people in their struggle for freedom.[18]

Although India's fight for independence was much different from the battle facing blacks, King came to believe nonviolence could overcome the brute force of racism. Indeed, King thought it was the only just way to achieve their rights because "the chain of hatred must be cut. When it is broken, brotherhood can begin."[19]

Graduate School and Marriage

King graduated from Crozer in May 1951 with a degree in divinity. Because King finished first in his class, he received a $1,300 scholarship for graduate school. In June he began attending Boston University to earn a doctor-ate in systematic theology, which he would receive on June 5, 1955.

King worked hard to get the advanced degree that would allow him to be called "Dr. King" for the rest of his life. His doctoral dissertation was titled "A Comparison of the Conceptions of God in the Thinking of Paul Tillich and Henry Nelson Weiman," two famous Protestant theologians. In addition to studying religion King also delved deeply into the ideas of many great political and social philosophers by taking additional courses at nearby Harvard University.

Although King was a hardworking student, he still found time for an active social life and dated frequently. While at Crozer, King even had a serious romance with a white woman, the daughter of the school's superintendent of buildings and grounds. Although the couple briefly thought about marriage, they broke up after they began to consider the serious problems they would face in an era in which most whites, and many blacks as well, disapproved of interracial marriage.

One of those who advised King to break off the romance was J. Pius Barbour, a black minister in Boston who befriended him and other black students. When Barbour confronted him about the relationship, King told him, "I'm glad you found out about it because we decided we wanted you to marry us!"[20] Barbour discussed the racism the couple would face and told

Coretta Scott King

Martin Luther King Jr. was a strong, proud person. So was the woman he married—Coretta Scott. They met in 1952 while both were attending school in Boston—King was doing graduate work at Boston University, and Scott was studying voice at the New England Conservatory of Music. In Martin Luther King Jr.: To The Mountaintop, *William Roger Witherspoon explains the family background that made Scott a strong, fearless partner for King during their long fight for civil rights:*

Coretta was a strong-willed young woman from Marion, Alabama, a rural community about eighty miles south of Montgomery. She was a farm girl—feeding hogs, picking cotton, tending crops, and carrying water from the well in the back yard. Both sets of grandparents owned three-hundred acre farms. Coretta had to walk four miles to the African Methodist Episcopal Zion Church on Sunday, and a bit farther each day to school, but at least the Scott kids didn't have to carry their one set of shoes and walk barefoot, like many of the other blacks in the region. In addition to farming, her father [Obadiah] hauled lumber with his own truck—something the poor whites in the area who could not afford trucks bitterly resented. "Sometimes they would stop him on a lonely road and curse him and threaten to kill him—and there was always a good chance they might do it," Coretta recalled. "But he used to say, 'If you look a white man in the eye, he can't hurt you.'" Still, he carried a pistol, and when he went back into the woods to find lumber he often told [his wife] Bernice, "I may not get back." Coretta grew up learning to live in fear for the lives of her family.

King bluntly that it would ruin his career as a black minister.

King did not become serious about anyone else until 1952, when he asked Mary Powell, a friend from Atlanta who lived in Boston, if she knew any southern girls he could date. Powell put him in contact with Coretta Scott, an Alabama native who was studying voice at Boston's New England Conservatory of Music. The daughter of a prosperous farmer in Alabama's Perry County, Coretta was an independent, beautiful young woman who valued education so much that she was working as a maid to help pay for her studies.

Coretta, however, almost refused to go out with King. The reason is that he was studying to be a Baptist minister. "I began to think of stereotypes of ministers I had known—fundamentalist in their thinking, very narrow, and

Martin Luther King hugs his wife, Coretta Scott King. The couple married in June 1953.

overly pious," she admitted.[21] But they did begin dating and fell in love. They were married June 18, 1953, by King's father on the lawn of the Scott home in Marion, Alabama.

Becoming a Pastor

By the time King married, he had already been working part-time for five years as an associate pastor at Ebeneezer Baptist Church, where he delivered some sermons and helped out in various activities when home from school. Although King had been ordained a minister on February 25, 1948, he had continued his education even though many black ministers did not have college degrees.

As King was finishing up his graduate work, he and Coretta began considering where to live. They enjoyed life in the North because they had more freedom. But despite the added racial problems they would face if they returned to the South, they both loved the area so much that King began looking for a job as a pastor in southern states.

In 1954 King applied for the position of pastor of Dexter Avenue Baptist Church in Montgomery, Alabama. When he won the job, the Kings were happy even though it meant a return to life under Jim Crow. One of the reasons they wanted to return home was that they sensed a new era, one that would mean that more freedom for blacks was about to begin. "We had the feeling," King wrote years later, "that something remarkable was unfolding in the South and we wanted to witness it."[22]

The Kings moved to Montgomery in the fall of 1954 so King could begin his new duties as pastor. It was in Montgomery that King would begin his transformation from Baptist minister to civil rights leader. It was there that he would not only witness history being made, as he had hoped, but would make it himself.

Chapter Two

THE MONTGOMERY BUS BOYCOTT

As a little boy Martin Luther King Jr. made his mother a promise one Sunday while a visiting preacher delivered an eloquent sermon. "Someday," he said, "I'm going to have me some big words like that."[23] In 1954 when King became pastor of Dexter Avenue Baptist Church in Montgomery, Alabama, he already had the words from his many years of education. In his weekly sermons King began to develop the dramatic style that would add power to those words.

Low-key and intellectual by nature, King had always been uncomfortable when black worshipers would punctuate sermons with loud chants of "Amen, Brother!" or rhythmic hand clapping. "I revolted against the emotionalism of Negro religion, the shouting and the stamping. I didn't understand it and it embarrassed me,"[24] King explained. Gradually, however, he began to enjoy the emotional bond he forged with his audience. As King became a master at adjusting his phrasing, the pace of his speech, and the tone of his voice to excite listeners, he realized those verbal tools could help him communicate important ideas about topics like racism, the greatest problem facing blacks:

And I tell you that any religion that professes to be concerned with the souls of men and is not concerned with the slums that damn them and the social conditions that cripple them is dry as dust religion. Religion deals with both heaven and earth, time and eternity, seeking not only to integrate man with God but man with man.[25]

Listeners reacted joyously to the drama and passion of King's sermons. His mighty words would soon reach far beyond Montgomery as he began the battle for civil rights that would consume the rest of his life.

Montgomery

King became Dexter Avenue's twentieth pastor on October 21, 1954. Although King was still finishing his doctoral thesis, King worked hard and began to impress his congregation and other blacks in Montgomery, the capital of Alabama and a rapidly growing community with a population of eighty thousand whites and fifty thousand blacks.

It was hard for Martin and Coretta to return to life in the South, where Jim Crow segregated the races and blacks were considered inferior. They had decided to come home because, like other blacks, they had new hope that segregation would soon end. It came from *Brown vs. Board of Education*, the landmark U.S. Supreme Court decision on May 17, 1954, which declared segregated schools unconstitutional because they denied blacks an equal opportunity for a quality education.

Despite the ruling, nothing changed in Alabama. The state board of education voted unanimously to continue segregation in the 1954–1955 school year. The state legislature approved a bill, which it claimed nullified the decision and would allow schools to remain segregated. This was bad news for the Kings—whose first child, Yolanda Denise, would be born on November 17, 1955—because segregated black schools provided inferior education.

In Alabama, however, the first important step toward ending segregation would not come in a schoolroom. It would happen aboard a bus, and it would vault King into national prominence.

Rosa Parks

One of the most annoying humiliations blacks endured was riding the Montgomery City Bus Lines. Blacks had to board the bus through the front door, pay their dime fare, get off, and reenter through the rear. Once aboard they were not allowed to sit in the first ten rows of seats, which were reserved for whites.

On the afternoon of Thursday, December 1, 1955, Rosa Parks was riding the Cleveland Avenue bus home after working as a seamstress at Montgomery Fair Department Store. She took a seat in the colored section, grateful to be off her feet after a tiring day. But when the bus became crowded, driver James F. Blake ordered blacks to give their seats to white passengers who had boarded after them. Several blacks did. But Parks, a small, neatly dressed, forty-two-year-old woman, stayed seated; she had paid a dime fare like the whites and believed she was entitled to her seat.

Blake walked back and told Parks to move, but she still refused. Blake told

Rosa Parks sits up front on a Montgomery bus in 1956. Parks's refusal in 1955 to give up her seat to a white passenger resulted in her arrest and inspired King to lead a boycott of the city's buses.

her, "I'm going to have you arrested," to which Parks replied calmly, "You may do that."[26] It was a brave response because Blake's words were no idle threat—Alabama bus drivers were empowered to enforce segregation laws. Blake called two policemen—F.B. Day and D.W. Mixona—who took Parks to jail.

Three other blacks had challenged the bus law that year and been arrested, but their cases had either been dismissed or they had been charged with disorderly conduct. This time officials made a tactical error by charging Parks with violating the city ordinance on segregated seating.

When E.D. Nixon, a union official with the Brotherhood of Sleeping Car Porters and a leader in the Montgomery and Alabama chapters of the National

Association for the Advancement of Colored People (NAACP) was notified of Parks's arrest, he was concerned: Parks and her husband were active in the NAACP, and he wanted to get her out of jail as soon as possible. But Nixon was also elated because of the charge filed against Parks. "This is what we've been waiting for," said Nixon, who knew the NAACP could now challenge the law's constitutional legality.[27]

Even though Nixon posted one hundred dollars bail for Parks, he felt the black community should do something more to protest her arrest. Nixon began phoning black leaders about an idea he had to boycott the buses. In his call to King, Nixon said,

We have been taking this type of thing too long already. I feel the time has come to boycott the buses. Only through a boycott can we make it clear to the white folks that we will not accept this type of treatment any longer.[28]

When King agreed, Nixon asked him if his church would host a meeting Friday night to discuss the situation. King said yes, and the next night about fifty people turned out to support a bus boycott. King and other blacks worked all weekend to spread the news of the protest. They printed thousands of fliers that explained Parks's arrest and sought support for a one-day bus boycott on Monday:

This [abuse of black bus riders] must be stopped. Negroes are citizens and have rights. Until we do something to stop these arrests, they will continue. The next time, it may be you. This woman's case will come up Monday. We are, therefore, asking every Negro to stay off the buses on Monday in protest of the arrest and trial. Don't ride the buses to work, to town, to school, or anywhere on Monday.[29]

No one knew if blacks would band together to make the boycott succeed. But on early Monday morning when the first scheduled bus passed the King residence, Coretta excitedly shouted: "Martin! Martin! Come quickly."[30] She was happy because the bus was empty. Montgomery blacks were fighting back.

King Becomes a Leader

Parks's trial on Monday lasted only five minutes. She was found guilty of violating a 1945 Alabama law on bus segregation and fined ten dollars and four dollars in court costs. The trial was over, but the fight for racial justice had only just begun.

That afternoon black leaders gathered to discuss what to do next. The boycott had been so successful that they decided to continue it, creating the Montgomery Improvement Association (MIA) to head the effort. The suggestion for the name came from the Reverend Ralph David Abernathy, pastor of First

Rosa Parks Tells Her Story

Rosa Parks is considered one of the great heroes of the Civil Rights movement because she had the courage one day to do a simple thing—she refused to give up the seat on a bus she had paid a dime to sit in. In Quiet Strength: The Faith, the Hope, and the Heart of a Woman Who Changed a Nation, *Rosa Parks explains the incident on December 1, 1955, which helped ignite a fight for black civil liberties:*

A white man got on, and the driver looked our way and said, "Let me have those seats." It did not seem proper, particularly for a woman, to give her seat to a man. All the passengers paid ten cents, just as he did. When more whites boarded the bus, the driver, J. P. Blake, ordered the blacks in the first row of the colored section (the row I was sitting in), to move to the rear. Bus drivers then had police powers, under both municipal and state laws, to enforce racial segregation. However, we were sitting in the section designated for colored. At first none of us moved. "Y'all better make it light on yourselves and let me have those seats," Blake said. Then three of the blacks in my row got up, but I stayed in my seat and slid closer to the window. I do not remember being frightened. But I sure did not believe I would "make it light" on myself by standing up. Our mistreatment was just not right, and I was tired of it. I knew someone had to take the first step. So I made up my mind not to move. Blake asked me if I was going to stand up. "No, I am not," I answered. Blake said that he would have to call the police. I said, "Go ahead." In less than five minutes, two policemen came and the driver pointed me out. He said that he wanted the seat and that I would not stand up. "Why do you push us around?" I said to one of the policemen. "I don't know," he answered, "but the law is the law and you're under arrest."

Montgomery's deputy sheriff fingerprints Rosa Parks after her arrest.

An empty city bus moves through downtown Montgomery. The Montgomery bus boycott was Martin Luther King's first use of the principle of nonviolent protest.

Baptist Church. MIA members then picked a president to lead the group—the unanimous choice was King.

Three weeks earlier, King had turned down an offer to head the local NAACP chapter, claiming he was new to the community. But King decided to take this position, saying, "Somebody has to do it and if you think I can, I will serve."[31] King was chosen for several reasons, including his impressive academic credentials and speaking ability, which would make a good impression on the public. Almost as important was that, as a newcomer, the twenty-six-year-old King did not have any past rivalries with other black leaders that could make them jealous of his new prominence.

At a rally that night, King told five thousand people: "You know, my friends, there comes a time when people get tired of being trampled over by the iron feet of oppression."[32] King then set forth the principle of nonviolence that would be at the heart of the bus boycott and future civil rights protests. He said MIA would refrain from the "violence and lawlessness" common in protests by the racist White Citizens' Council, which burned crosses and beat blacks who angered them, and he promised that Montgomery blacks would triumph because they were in the right:

Now, let us say that we are not here advocating violence, we have overcome that. I want it to be known throughout Montgomery and throughout this nation that we are—a *Christian* people. But the great glory of American democracy is the right to protest for right. And if we are wrong, the Supreme Court of this nation is wrong. If we are wrong, God Almighty is wrong![33]

King had been anxious about how his speech would be received. But King's magnificent words, in an address only sixteen minutes long, ended to thunderous applause. The speech washed away his personal fears and signaled the arrival of a powerful new civil rights leader.

King Heads the Movement

On December 8 King explained to reporters that MIA was not seeking "an end to segregation. That's a matter for the legislature and the courts."[34] Instead the boycott that began December 5 and would last 382 days began with more modest goals: courteous treatment for black riders and a promise that the city consider hiring black bus drivers on black routes.

When Mayor W.A. "Tacky" Gayle and other officials rejected the requests, King and the MIA prepared for a long boycott, one they knew could economically hurt the bus line because blacks provided 75 percent of its revenue. The

Martin Luther King addresses a group of civil rights activists. A persuasive and dynamic speaker, King used his talent as an orator to rally supporters to his cause.

problem facing MIA was how thousands of blacks too poor to own cars could get around without the bus. The solution was a car pooling network that utilized volunteers to drive people to work, the doctor, and other places in vehicles that were either privately owned or purchased by MIA and local churches.

King helped plan this volunteer network and sometimes served as a driver. King also became the official spokesman for the protest movement. He did a good job explaining the situation to reporters, who came away impressed with his intelligence and the eloquent way he expressed himself. The celebrity King gained from media coverage helped him fulfill another duty—raising thousands of dollars MIA needed each month to pay for free rides and other expenses. King traveled around the country to give speeches and secure contributions.

King was also a key figure in planning boycott strategy. When the city refused to negotiate terms to end the tense situation, King and others realized the only solution was to challenge the racist bus law's legality. On February 2, MIA filed suit in federal court declaring that the law was unconstitutional. The basis of the challenge was the Fourteenth Amendment to the U.S. Constitution, which was ratified in 1868 to protect the rights of blacks, most of whom had been freed from slavery after the Civil War. The amendment reads:

No State shall make or enforce any law which shall abridge the privileges or immunities of citizens of the United States; nor shall any State deprive any person of life, liberty, or property, without due process of law; nor deny to any person within its jurisdiction the equal protection of the law.[35]

The amendment had not been used extensively in the twentieth century to protect black rights, but it now became a strong weapon against segregation. While the legal challenge worked its way through state and federal courts, Montgomery blacks had to contend with the wrath of angry whites.

White Backlash

One of the first victims of white anger was Parks, who on January 7, 1956, was fired from her job. Although Parks called it "a blessing in a way, because I didn't have to worry about how I was going to get to and from work without riding the buses,"[36] it was only one small way in which whites tried to intimidate King and other blacks so they could keep them powerless by denying them their rights.

Although the initial MIA requests had been moderate, Montgomery officials rejected them because they felt they were a direct assault on segregation, which was at the heart of southern life. "The white people," claimed Mayor Gayle, "are firm in their convictions that they do not care whether the Negroes ever ride a city bus again if it means that the social fabric of our community is to be destroyed."[37] Jack Crenshaw, a lawyer for the bus company, was more honest. He admitted officials feared that if they gave in to black demands, "Negroes would go about boasting they had won a victory over the white people, and this we will not stand for."[38]

Elected officials tried to stop the boycott. Initially, black taxi cab owners offered rides for ten cents, the same price as a bus ticket. City officials ended that by threatening to enforce a city ordinance that set a forty-five-cent minimum cab fare. Police also harassed blacks waiting to be picked up by car pools, stopped car-pool vehicles to check for safety problems, and issued tickets for imaginary traffic violations.

On February 21, 1956, the Montgomery County Grand Jury charged

Many Whites Hated Blacks

The white backlash to the attempt by blacks in Montgomery, Alabama, to win the simple right to ride a bus without being discriminated against was not unexpected. But the brutal ugliness of the racism that generated this response is hard to understand even today. In Walls Come Tumbling Down: A History of the Civil Rights Movement 1940–1970, *author Thomas R. Brooks includes passages from a leaflet the Association of White Citizens' Councils distributed to publicize a February 10, 1956, rally against the bus boycott. The main speaker to the crowd of twelve thousand was James Eastland, a U.S. senator. The leaflet was headlined "LET'S GET ON THE BALL WHITE CITIZENS." It openly, and in crude racist terms, advocated whites to use violence to control blacks:*

When in the course of human events it becomes necessary to abolish the Negro race, proper methods should be used. Among these are guns, bow and arrows, sling shots and knives.

We hold these truths to be self-evident: that all whites are created equal with certain rights; among these are life, liberty and the pursuit of dead niggers.

In every stage of the bus boycott we have been oppressed and degraded because of [blacks].

My friends it is time we wised up to those black devils. I tell you there are a group of two legged agitators who persist in walking up and down our streets protruding their black lips. If we don't stop helping these African flesh eaters [cannibals], we will soon wake up and find Reverend King in the White House.

King and eighty-eight other MIA leaders with violating an obscure Alabama law once used to restrict labor strikes. The law made it illegal for groups to prevent the operation of a business without just cause. Within forty-eight hours, King and the others were arrested, and on March 22 King was found guilty and fined five hundred dollars. No one else was tried because King's conviction was appealed; the boycott ended before his appeal was decided.

White citizens held rallies to support segregation. Some whites, many of them members of racist groups like the Ku Klux Klan, tried to scare blacks. They jeered at blacks while driving past them and sometimes beat them up. They also fired guns at buses and cars carrying blacks and bombed churches and homes.

Targeting King

As head of the MIA, King was a key target. On January 26 two motorcycle policemen stopped King for driving five miles an hour too fast in a twenty-five-mile-per-hour zone. Although speeders were not normally arrested, King was taken to jail, a frightening experience for southern blacks because white jailers often beat them. King also began to receive death threats in the mail and by telephone.

One night when King was troubled by his fears that angry whites might strike at his family, he got up, had a cup of coffee, and began praying. King explains what happened during his talk with God:

I experienced the presence of the Divine as I have never experienced Him before. It seemed as though I could hear the quiet assurances of an inner voice saying: "Stand up for righteousness, stand up for truth, and God will be at your side forever." Almost at once my fears began to go.[39]

King would soon need that serenity. Three nights later, on January 30, which ironically was Mohandas Gandhi's birthday, King was at a rally at First Baptist Church when a bomb exploded at his home. Although the sticks of dynamite thrown on his porch caused some damage, Coretta and their infant daughter, Yolanda, were uninjured. When King rushed home, Coretta told him of a telephone call she received after the bomb went off: "Yes, I did it," said a woman. "And I'm just sorry I didn't kill all you bastards."[40]

The message was one of mindless hate. The mood of several hundred blacks who gathered at King's home was also one of anger and violence; many wanted to get guns and attack whites in revenge. King calmed them down by repeating his message of nonviolence:

We must love our white brothers no matter what they do to us. We must

Martin Luther and Coretta Scott King leave an Alabama courthouse in March 1956. King was subjected to court battles, police harassment, and violence during his civil rights campaign in Montgomery.

make them know that we love them. Jesus still cries out across the centuries: "Love your enemies." We must learn to meet hate with love.[41]

Victory at Last

Despite the violence and difficult conditions they faced, Montgomery blacks continued their boycott for over a year while the lawsuit on segregated buses slowly made its way through the legal system. On June 5, 1956, a federal court in Alabama ruled the law unconstitutional because it discriminated against blacks. Alabama officials appealed, but on November 13, 1956, the U.S. Supreme Court upheld the decision.

King got the good news while in a Montgomery courtroom. King was attending a hearing on a lawsuit the city had filed to stop the car pools, claiming the independent operation was a public nuisance. The high court decision rendered the hearing moot—Montgomery blacks had won and no longer needed the car pool.

Montgomery Blacks Help Each Other

The bus boycott created a severe problem for many blacks because they did not own cars. The solution the Montgomery Improvement Association (MIA) came up with was a mass carpooling effort to give people rides wherever they had to go. In Martin Luther King: To The Mountaintop, *William Roger Witherspoon describes this effort, which had an unexpected benefit of helping to pull the black community together during the crisis:*

By Tuesday, December 13 [1955], the entire car-pool system was laid out, with most of the forty-eight dispatch points being in black churches, which provided the advantage of seating and warmth on cold mornings. There were another forty-two pickup points in white areas, and mimeographed maps of the city showing the locations of each were circulated through the black community. King, [Jo Ann] Robinson, and many of the leaders with cars participated in the car pool fairly regularly, and a number of students volunteered to drive cars virtually full time. Fifteen of the black churches bought station wagons and painted the name of their church on the side so they officially became church vehicles, which were constantly picking up people for "church business." The young boycott was having a dramatic effort on the divided black community of Montgomery. For the first time, the poor and uneducated worked together in a common effort with the black professionals. Blacks who never rode the buses now shared cars and long walks with those who had never owned automobiles. Pharmacists and physicians used their stores and waiting rooms as pickup points, their phones as dispatch centers. Black morticians transported the living to their places of work before taking the dead to their place of rest. And the MIA employed twenty-five people as full-time drivers.

The next night King told a gathering of several thousand blacks that the boycott was over. He warned them not to brag about the victory but to return to riding buses "with humility and meekness" even though it had been a hard-won triumph: "Our feet have often been tired and our automobiles worn, but we have kept going with the faith that in our struggle we had cosmic companionship [God] and that, at bottom, the universe is on the side of justice."[42]

When Montgomery buses were integrated on December 21, King and E.D. Nixon rode the city's first bus. The story *New York Times* reporter George Barrett wrote that historic day described a humorous interchange between black and white riders:

> Two white men in one bus found themselves sitting behind a Negro, and one of the men said, "I see this sure isn't going to be a white Christmas [referring to a lack of snow]." The Negro looked up, and smiled. He said with good humor but firmness, "Yes, sir, that's right." Everybody in the bus smiled, and all rancor seemed to evaporate.[43]

Some whites were furious that blacks had won and began a campaign of violence against blacks. Racist whites beat a teenage girl after she got off a bus, shot a pregnant woman in the legs, and fired a shotgun blast through King's front door. On January 10, when King and Abernathy were in Atlanta for a meeting of southern black ministers, whites bombed and destroyed several churches and homes, including those of Abernathy.

King's Expectations

The violence bothered King. But following the victory, he was also concerned that his sudden personal success was so overwhelming that he would never be able to equal it again. He told a friend, J. Pius Barbour,

> I'm worried to death. A man who hits the peak at twenty-seven [with the victory in Montgomery] has a tough job ahead. People will be expecting me to pull rabbits out of a hat for the rest of my life.[44]

King should not have worried. He would soon ascend to new heights and become the nation's top civil rights leader.

Chapter Three

King Becomes a National Leader

The victory in Montgomery, Alabama, was significant because it emboldened other southern blacks to challenge segregation laws. By the time buses there were integrated, similar protests had begun in Birmingham and Mobile, Alabama, and Tallahassee, Florida. Equally as important historically for the revitalized Civil Rights movement was that Martin Luther King Jr. emerged as the symbolic head of the renewed fight for black rights.

The boycott's national news coverage had swiftly transformed King from an unknown Baptist minister to one of the most recognized blacks in America. As president of the Montgomery Improvement Association (MIA), King was quoted in hundreds of stories in newspapers and magazines, and millions of people saw his face and heard

his voice in nightly television news reports.

As the boycott dragged on, King had also begun making speeches across the country to tell "The Montgomery Story" and to raise funds; during the boycott, MIA needed $225,000 for expenses such as the legal challenge to the law and the car pool. King's message was a powerful one for both whites and blacks:

Integration is the great issue of our age, the great issue of our nation and the great issue of our community. We are in the midst of a great struggle, the consequence of which will be world shaking.[45]

King's popularity grew dramatically because he appealed to both whites and blacks. African Americans admired

King for his courage in fighting racism. Whites were impressed as well by his high academic achievements, his dignified manner, and the intelligent, poised way he expressed himself. On February 18, 1957, *Time* magazine cemented his growing celebrity by putting him on its cover and lavishly praising him in a long story. Author Lee Griggs wrote of King,

> Personally humble, articulate, and of high educational attainment, Martin Luther King Jr. is, in fact, what many a Negro—and were it not for his color, many a white would like to be.[46]

A New Black Spokesman

Biographer Lerone Bennett Jr. claims that the fame King acquired in Montgomery helped him develop "a popular backing of a depth and intensity unknown in America since the

Why King Became So Popular

There are many reasons why Martin Luther King Jr. became not only a well-known civil rights leader but one who was deeply admired by whites as well as by blacks. In The Civil Rights Movement and the People Who Made It, *author Fred Powledge quotes James Farmer, the founder of the Congress of Racial Equality, on why King appealed to so many different kinds of people:*

> King did have a combination of qualities. He was a southern Baptist preacher, speaking with a southern accent—that was important [to blacks]—who could *preach*. He could make 'em shout [with fiery sermons]. And that, too, was important. At the same time, he could address a Harvard [University] audience and do it intelligently. Quite a rare combination. There are many Baptist preachers who can make them shout, but how many of them can speak to Harvard at the same time? How many of them at that date—1955, 1956—knew of [Mohandas] Gandhi and Gandhi's work and could speak of nonviolence?

Powledge also notes that much has been written about the fact that King almost seemed to have been accidentally thrust into the position of a national leader by the events he was involved in. Again he quotes Farmer, who claims King relished his position, however he obtained it: "A reluctant knight? Well, yes, there was a bit of that, but not as much as you think, no. He enjoyed it, too."

days of Booker T. Washington."[47] He became one of only a handful of blacks who had gained national stature since the end of the Civil War, which freed blacks from slavery but not the consequences of racism.

Until King no black leader had been as admired throughout America as Washington, who was born a slave in 1856. Washington became the nation's best-known black spokesman in the post–Civil War era by making Alabama's Tuskegee Institute a quality school of higher education for blacks. Washington also advised blacks that—at least in the final decades of the nineteenth century—it was still wiser to tolerate segregation and other injustices so they could live peacefully with whites.

King was actually closer in philosophy and background to W.E.B. Du Bois, a more fiery leader, born in 1868, who was the first black to earn a master's degree from Harvard University and a cofounder of the National Association for the Advancement of Colored People (NAACP). In the first years of the twentieth century, Du Bois harshly criticized Washington's willingness to let whites dominate them and told blacks to stand up for their rights. In *The Souls of Black Folk*, his most famous work, Du Bois in 1903 prophesied, "The problem of the Twentieth Century is the problem of the colorline."[48] That famous quote was echoed in King's own oft-repeated claim that integration was still the nation's most serious problem more than a half-century later.

Although King respected other black leaders who came before him, he developed his own philosophy, goals, and tactics. In a book about King's cultural legacy, Lewis V. Baldwin labels King "the great synthesizer" because he borrowed ideas from so many previous leaders:

Like his predecessors, King not only challenged evil and unjust systems with words but with militant and sustained action as well. King reflected the spirit of [Washington] by stressing the importance of exercising restraint when necessary and working with the system as much as possible. He accepted the appeal [of leaders like Du Bois] for black unity and militant, assertive action.[49]

In 1957 King completed his ascension to power as one of the most respected black leaders in America. He did this by creating a powerful new group to fight segregation.

Founding SCLC

The Montgomery victory sparked a growing interest among southern blacks to continue this new offensive against segregation in their communities. King now used the fame and influence he had acquired to support and coordinate such efforts.

On January 10, 1957, King and Ralph David Abernathy, a Baptist

Booker T. Washington vs. W.E.B. Du Bois

Two of the greatest black leaders before Martin Luther King Jr. were Booker T. Washington and W.E.B. Du Bois. In the last two decades of the nineteenth century Washington, born a slave, headed Tuskegee Institute, which trained blacks for skilled jobs such as carpentry. Washington believed blacks should try to get along with whites even though they did not treat blacks as equals. Du Bois was more militant and wanted blacks to stand up and fight for those rights. King learned from both leaders. The following quotations from Washington and Du Bois explain their differing philosophies. They are taken from The Black Americans: A History in Their Own Words 1619–1983, *which was edited by Milton Meltzer.*

In a famous speech at the Cotton States Exposition in Atlanta, Georgia, in 1895, Washington explained his views on black-white relations:

In all things that are purely social, we can be separate as the fingers, yet one as the hand in all things essential to mutual progress. The wisest among my race understand that the agitation of questions of social equality is the extremest folly, and that progress in the enjoyment of all the privileges [rights] that will come to us must be the result of severe and constant struggle rather than of artificial forcing. It is important and right that all privileges of the law be ours, but it is vastly more important that we be prepared for the exercise of those privileges.

Du Bois criticized Washington, and in An ABC of Color *he wrote that blacks should demand full equality in areas like education and economic opportunity:*

We will not be satisfied to take one jot or tittle less than our full manhood rights. We claim for ourselves every single right that belongs to a freeborn American, political, civil and social; and until we get these rights we will never cease to protest and assail the ears of America. . . . How shall we get them? By voting where we may vote, by persistent, unceasing agitation, by hammering at the truth, by sacrifice and work.

W.E.B Du Bois (left) and Booker T. Washington had very different beliefs about how to pursue equal rights for black people.

minister from Montgomery who during the boycott had become his right-hand man, were in Atlanta, Georgia, to organize a new group to help southern blacks. But early that morning, they learned that Abernathy's home and church were among several that had been bombed in the wave of violence that followed the bus integration. And on January 27 twelve sticks of dynamite, which failed to explode but were still smoldering, were discovered on King's front porch.

The attacks did not stop King and Abernathy. Along with representatives of sixty religious, civil rights, and civic groups, they went ahead in their meeting on January 10 and January 11 to form the Southern Leadership Conference on Transportation and Nonviolent Integration. The group's unwieldy name was changed the next month in New Orleans to the Southern Christian Leadership Conference (SCLC).

King's new fame and the ability he had shown in Montgomery made him a natural choice for SCLC president; he would head it until his death in 1968. Nonviolent protest had secured the victory in Montgomery, and King brought that tactic to SCLC. The group adopted a slogan that summed up this philosophy: "Not one hair of one head of one white person shall be harmed."[50]

Prayer Pilgrimage
SCLC gave King a formal platform to fight racism. It also made him the equal of other national black leaders such as NAACP executive secretary Roy Wilkins and Asa P. Randolph, who headed the Brotherhood of Black Sleeping Car Porters and had been a major force in the civil rights fight for decades.

The Montgomery boycott brought new strength to the fight for black rights, and Wilkins and Randolph wanted to build on that by holding a mass protest in Washington, D.C., the nation's capital. They met with King in New York in March to plan the Prayer Pilgrimage. It was held May 17, 1957, the third anniversary of the Supreme Court decision outlawing segregated schools, and King stole the spotlight during the daylong round of speeches at the Lincoln Monument.

Draped in the black robe of a Baptist minister, King drew the loudest applause and the most fervent shouts of "Amen!" from the crowd of fifteen thousand during his speech. King's main theme was that the only way blacks could secure their rights was to increase their political power by having more of them vote in elections:

Give us the ballot! Give us the ballot and we will no longer have to worry [ask] the federal government about our basic rights. We will no longer plead—we will write the proper laws on the books. Give us the ballot, and we will fill the legislatures with men of good will. Give

Martin Luther King speaks to thousands during the Prayer Pilgrimage, a rally in Washington, D.C., to celebrate the third anniversary of the Supreme Court decision to outlaw school segregation.

us the ballot, and we will get the people judges who love mercy.[51]

King's solution to black ills, however, could only come after a prolonged battle. Although voting is a right guaranteed every citizen, southern elected officials—which in that era meant only white officials—made it difficult, sometimes almost impossible, for blacks to register to vote. Jim Crow laws forced blacks to take a literacy test that included questions almost no one could answer or to pay a poll tax so high that almost no one could afford it. At this point in history only 28 percent of blacks in the South were registered to vote compared to 70 percent in the

North; this included only 4 percent in Mississippi.

If any doubts had existed on whether or not King deserved the status of a national leader, his dynamic performance at the Prayer Pilgrimage dispelled them. King received the lion's share of news coverage and was lavishly praised. James L. Hicks of the *Amsterdam News*, an influential New York black newspaper, proclaimed King "the number one leader of sixteen million Negroes in the United States. At this point in his career, the people will follow him anywhere."[52]

Not Much Government Help

The Prayer Pilgrimage had an immediate impact by building support for the Civil Rights Act of 1957, which received final approval in the Senate on August 23 despite a twenty-nine-hour filibuster by Senator Strom Thurmond, who believed in segregation. The measure was the first civil rights bill in eighty-two years. Although it created the Civil Rights Commission to investigate laws that kept blacks from voting, the bill was weak because it did not include any measures to enforce the law when irregularities were discovered. And King and other black leaders soon found out that southern whites were still not ready to treat them equally unless forced to by the government.

In September, just weeks after the bill passed, Arkansas governor Orval Faubus ordered the state National Guard to prevent nine black students from enrolling at Little Rock High School, even though the federal court had issued an order allowing them to attend. President Dwight Eisenhower had to assume federal control of the National Guard to prevent Faubus from defying the order.

Despite Eisenhower's historic step to enforce integration, he did not act aggressively to protect black rights in other situations. His administration reluctantly enforced court orders on desegregation, which blacks had won through long, involved legal battles, and it would not act on its own to protect such rights.

On June 23, 1958, King, Wilkins, Randolph, and Lester B. Granger of the Urban League met with Eisenhower to ask him to make the U.S. Justice Department actively enforce equal rights. When the meeting broke up, Eisenhower had only vague assurances for them. Referring to other difficult issues he faced, such as dealing with the Soviet Union in the Cold War, Eisenhower muttered to King as he left, "Reverend, there are so many problems."[53] The president seemed to be apologizing, in advance, for his inability to help blacks.

Trumpeting His Message

Because the federal government was slow to force southern states to treat blacks fairly, King believed the best way to weaken racism's grip on the

South was to build support for the cause of racial equality nationally. While SCLC began to help blacks challenge segregation laws, King used his new fame and popularity to travel the country, and even the world, to convince people such change was needed.

In 1957 King crisscrossed the nation, traveling 780,000 miles in America and other countries and delivering 208 speeches as he sought to make white and black leaders join the fight against racism. His speeches cast the plight of blacks in almost biblical terms, and King's dramatic delivery always impressed his audience. "For too long have we been trampled under the iron feet of oppression, too long bound in the starless midnight of racism,"

King's View of the Black Struggle

In What Manner of Man *Lerone Bennett Jr. explains the attitude that Martin Luther King Jr. developed about the fight for black rights. Bennett wrote:*

As a result of his immersion in the church of fire [the Montgomery bus boycott], King had come to radically different conclusions about the nature of the Negro struggle [than previous black leaders]. A key concept in his new orientation was the idea of confrontation, the idea of bringing out into the open submerged evils, of *forcing* face-to-face meetings of man and man, of community and community, individually as in the refusal of a single individual to accept segregation, collectively as in the open challenge by a Negro community of the [orders] and fears of a white community. The idea that nothing substantial would happen in the field of race relations if men and communities were not *forced* to face evils was started with great eloquence by Asa Randolph in the forties, but King carried it to a higher stage of development, making the "showdown situation" the central component of the Negro's new vision of battle. Like Randolph, he believed direct action indispensable for racial progress. "Pressure, even conflict," he said, "was an unfortunate but necessary element in social change. Abandoning the mainstream Negro leadership tradition, which shied away from conflict and considered direct appeals to the masses inflammatory, King called for a total mobilization of all the resources in the Negro community. He stressed, moreover, the responsibility of every individual to history in the making. Every individual, according to King, had a right, nay, a duty, to break or ignore unjust laws. Any man who accepted segregation involved himself, tragically, in his own degradation.

King would say to applause from whites and shouts of "Amen!" from blacks.[54]

He also wrote *Stride Toward Freedom*, which told the story of the Montgomery boycott. It was while promoting the book on September 20, 1957, that King was almost killed when a mentally ill black woman, Izola Curry, stabbed him in the chest while he was signing copies of the book in a New York City department store. Although the wound was serious and King was hospitalized for several days,

Martin Luther King recovers in a New York hospital after being stabbed by a mentally ill woman in 1957.

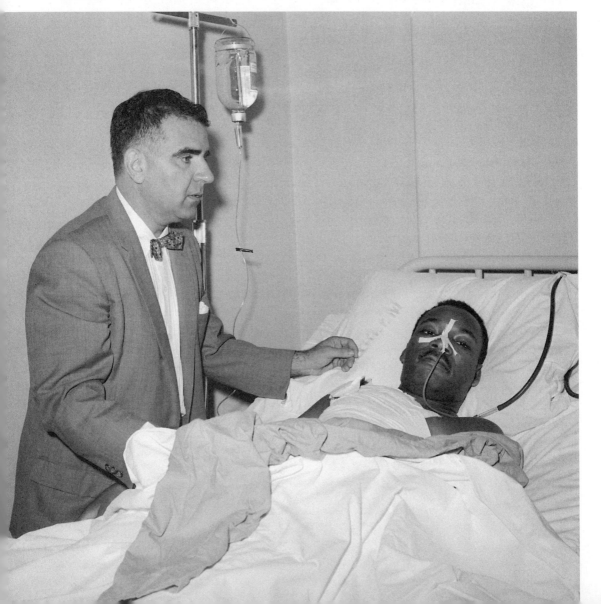

he did not want Curry charged. "Coretta," he told his wife, "this woman needs help. She is not responsible for the violence. Don't do anything to her, don't prosecute, get her healed."[55]

King had two goals in writing the book—to educate whites about the problems blacks faced and to guide blacks in staging similar assaults on segregation. King wrote that the injustice done to blacks in Montgomery "is merely symptomatic of the larger national problem [of racism]," which he believed could destroy America if left unresolved:

> Every crisis has both its dangers and opportunities. It can spell either salvation or doom. In the present crisis America can achieve either racial justice or the ultimate social psychosis that can only lead to domestic suicide.[56]

His message was a harsh one for whites, many of whom preferred to ignore such a serious problem. But by confronting them with the issue, King was able to make more people aware of the need to change the inhumane conditions that still existed for southern blacks.

World Traveler

King traveled to other countries, like Ghana in Africa, to spread his message, and in February 1959 he took a trip that had great personal meaning. King went to India so he could more deeply study Mohandas Gandhi's techniques of nonviolence, which he had already adopted in battling racism. "To other countries I may go as a tourist," King said, "but to India I come as a pilgrim."[57] King returned home on March 19 more convinced than ever that nonviolent protest was the key to winning civil rights battles.

Although King traveled and spoke extensively, he did not ignore SCLC. He was not involved with the group on a daily basis, but he contributed his speaking fees to fund its operations and helped plan its activities. SCLC's top priority was voter registration; in 1958 it held twenty-one mass meetings in key southern cities to get blacks to register. SCLC also continued working in the area of public transportation, with a major victory coming in 1959 when Atlanta buses were desegregated.

In late 1959 King resigned as pastor of Dexter Avenue Baptist Church and moved to Atlanta so he could work on a daily basis with SCLC. King, whose family had grown to four on October 23, 1957, with the birth of a son, Martin Luther King III, also became copastor of Ebeneezer Baptist, the church his father headed.

Striking Back at King

As King's fame and leadership role in civil rights grew, he became a target for whites who feared he would be successful in overturning segregation. Police and other government officials

King Is Stabbed

One of the most frightening incidents that happened to Martin Luther King Jr. came on September 20, 1958, when he was signing copies of Stride Toward Freedom *in a New York City department store. Izola Curry, a mentally ill black woman, attacked King, stabbing him in the chest. The wound was life threatening—doctors told King that if the knife had been jostled while it was still in his chest, even if he had just sneezed, it could have pierced his heart and killed him—and he spent several days in the hospital recovering. In* The Days of Martin Luther King, Jr., *author Jim Bishop describes this dramatic event at what should have been a triumphant personal appearance for King:*

Inside [Blumstein's Department Store] he sat alone at a desk, smiling at a line of women—mostly black—who held copies of his book. One woman, however, ignored the line. She walked to the desk and said softly, "Are you Dr. King?" He looked up from the book and grinned, "Yes, I am." The expression on the woman's face changed swiftly. "You son of a bitch!" she screamed, and took a long Japanese letter opener from her purse. "Luther King," she shouted, "I've been after you for years!" The blade came down hard, tore through the white shirt and into his ribs until only the handle was sticking from his chest. King sat quietly, knowing what danger there was in moving [the blade could have pierced his heart]. The others waiting, in line, began to scream. His attacker ran for the front door but was stopped by employees. Another woman, shrieking hysterically, tried to pull the letter opener from Dr. King's chest. He turned pleading eyes on her, motioning her not to do it. A store employee slowly removed the woman's hand from the blade.

made up phony charges so they could arrest him, and he also began receiving more death threats.

On September 3, 1958, King was roughly taken into custody by two officers for allegedly refusing to obey their order to leave when he tried to enter the Montgomery Recorder's Court to attend a friend's hearing. Bond for the minor offense was set at one hundred thousand dollars. When he was convicted the next day after pleading not guilty to a reduced charge of loitering, Montgomery police commissioner Clyde C. Sellers, over King's objections, paid his small fine. Sellers claimed King had engineered the arrest to create headlines, when actually the police officers had made up the charge so they could jail him.

On February 17, 1960, Alabama officials issued a warrant charging King with lying on his 1956 and 1958 tax returns; two Fulton County (Georgia) deputy sheriffs arrested him that same day in Atlanta. It was the first time Alabama had prosecuted anyone for perjury in a tax filing, and it was obvious it was done to harass King out of spite for his having integrated Montgomery buses.

Alabama officials claimed King had made personal use of funds he had helped raise for the boycott, which meant he made more money those years than he stated he did. It was a phony charge. Even though an all-white jury found King innocent on May 28, Coretta said the incident "caused him more suffering than any other event of his life up to that point"[58] because it questioned something dear to him—his personal honesty.

Southern officials kept looking for ways to punish King. On October 19, 1960, they arrested King and fifty-one other people for trespassing during a protest at a segregated diner in Rich's, an Atlanta department store. The others were quickly released on bail, but King was taken before Judge Oscar Mitchell, who two months earlier had sentenced him to a year in jail for driving in Georgia with Alabama license plates; King had forgotten to get new plates when he moved to Atlanta.

The sentence had been suspended, but because of the new violation the judge ordered King to serve four months in prison. On October 26 after the police drove King to Reidsville State Prison, King wrote a letter to Coretta saying, "This is the cross that we must bear for the freedom of our people."[59]

Kennedy Helps

King did not remain in prison long. Two days later Mitchell freed King on two thousand dollars bail even though he had originally denied King bail. Mitchell changed his mind due to the

Robert Kennedy helped secure King's release from jail in October 1960.

intercession of John F. Kennedy, a Massachusetts senator running for president, and his brother, Robert. When John heard King had been arrested, he called Coretta to see if there was anything he could do. The next day Robert telephoned Mitchell and argued that King should be released for what was a minor offense. Mitchell caved in to Robert, who in a few months would become U.S. attorney general when John was elected president.

The telephone call is one of the most famous in presidential politics, and Daddy King and other black leaders began urging African Americans to vote for Kennedy. A famous quote attributed to King Sr.—"I've got all my votes and I've got a suitcase, and I'm going to take them up there and dump them in his lap"[60]—sums up the effect that Kennedy's call had on the presidential race. Kennedy defeated Richard M. Nixon by the razor thin margin of 112,000 votes, and many believe that the overwhelming majority Kennedy had in black votes was at least partially attributed to his act of kindness toward King.

A New Era

The incident involving King and Kennedy foreshadowed the dramatic incidents that would take place in the next few years in the battle for civil rights, events that would involve both of these historic figures. Kennedy's election meant there was finally a president willing to act to protect black rights.

Just as Kennedy had stepped in to help free King, he would now use the power of his new office to further the fight for racial equality for all blacks. And King would again be at the forefront of this battle, reaching new heights of fame and leadership.

Chapter Four

KING PURSUES HIS DREAM OF RACIAL JUSTICE

Martin Luther King Jr. moved home to Atlanta, Georgia, to revitalize the Southern Christian Leadership Conference (SCLC). Despite some small victories in increasing the numbers of black voters and weakening segregation's bitter hold, SCLC had not radically improved life for southern blacks. But on December 1, 1959, King predicted the Civil Rights movement was about to enter a more active phase:

> The time has come for a broad, bold advance of the Southern campaign for equality. After prayerful consideration, I am convinced that the psychological moment has come when a concentrated drive against injustice can bring great tangible gains. We must not let the present strategic opportunity pass.[61]

King's prophesy would come true—the decade of the 1960s would see great triumphs for blacks. King, however, would share center stage with new combatants in the civil rights battle—brave young college students who started to sweep away the humiliating Jim Crow laws that had segregated blacks since the Civil War.

Sit-in Protests

On February 1, 1960, Joseph McNeil, an eighteen-year-old North Carolina Agricultural and Technical State College student, made history by sitting down at a Woolworth's lunch counter in Greensboro, North Carolina, and ordering a cup of coffee. "We don't serve colored in here," a white waitress said, to which McNeil responded, "We'll sit here until we're served."[62]

Joseph McNeil (left) and three other men stage a sit-in protest at a Greensboro, North Carolina, lunch counter. The 1960 sit-in inspired more than one hundred such protests in cities across the South.

McNeil and three other students—Ezell Blair Jr., Franklin McCain, and David Richmond—had just begun the first of scores of sit-in protests throughout the South.

The four remained seated until the store closed at 5:30 P.M. They returned the next day with about twenty students and occupied most of the stools in the small whites-only restaurant. Even though they kept getting arrested, students and other blacks kept coming back day after day and sitting down politely to protest segregation.

Sit-ins were not a new tactic; the Congress of Racial Equality (CORE) had pioneered them in 1942, and in 1958 black youths had staged them in Kansas and Oklahoma. But as King had prophesied, the time had come for such dramatic action to be accepted. News reports spread the story of the protests; by the following week similar sit-ins were under way in more than thirteen cities in four states, and within a year they would spread to over one hundred communities.

Hundreds of demonstrators were arrested on charges such as trespassing

Victory in Nashville

The lunch counter protests that spread quickly throughout the South in the early 1960s were usually peaceful events. However, whites who opposed integration sometimes fought back with violence. In Martin Luther King: To The Mountaintop, *author William Roger Witherspoon explains one such incident in Nashville, Tennessee:*

The Nashville [Student Nonviolent Coordinating Committee (SNCC)] was perhaps the most organized of all the student movements, the result of nearly a year of nonviolent training by [Reverend James Lawson, who had worked with King]. Throughout the spring, the students from Fisk, Meharry, Tennessee State, and the Seminary had been filling up the city's jails and tying up downtown—taking the thirty days [sentence] instead of paying the thirty-dollar fine. On April 18, the home of Alexander Luby, the students' attorney, was destroyed by a bomb. Furious, Diane Nash and C.T. Vivian led five thousand students to city hall. A beleaguered Mayor Ben West came out to talk to them—he wasn't about to order the police to try and disperse that many. "The students were mad," said [SNCC leader John] Lewis, "and Diane was a contrast on the city hall steps with her calm, cool manner. And she asked the mayor point blank, 'Do you favor the desegregation of the lunch counters and restaurants.' And the mayor looked at the crowd and said, 'Yes, young lady, I favor the integration of the lunch counters and restaurants.'" He had publicly capitulated, and resistance crumbled. Within two weeks, downtown Nashville was integrated; the first major victory for the student movement.

Martin Luther King speaks in Nashville. The integration of lunch counters and restaurants in Nashville was the first major victory for SNCC.

and disorderly conduct, and many spent weeks in jail. But historian Anthony Lewis writes that "the sit-ins were an immediate success" and brought positive results quickly: "It took just six months to open the counter at Woolworth's in Greensboro to all races. Hundreds of other stores [in the South] began serving Negroes by the end of 1960 and hundreds more in succeeding years."[63]

King's Influence

Even though King did not initiate sit-ins, historians consider him their spiritual father because participants adopted the tactics of nonviolence he pioneered in Montgomery. Their willingness to break unjust laws also followed a philosophy King voiced following the boycott: "Every man has a right and personal responsibility to break, ignore and resist certain local laws—no matter what the personal consequences are—in order to abide by the national law."[64]

King supported the new tactic because he understood it was exactly what was needed to push the civil rights battle to a new level. Biographer Lerone Bennett Jr. writes,

The sit-ins, as King realized almost immediately, were the real turning point in race relations in America. Montgomery had been a stride toward rebellion; Greensboro and the cities beyond were rebellion itself. King watched, fascinated,

recognizing in it the fruit of his own efforts and the fruit of his dreams.[65]

He even offered his help to the fledgling movement. Because he knew the string of protests could falter without a formal organization to guide them, King invited students to meet at Shaw University in Raleigh, North Carolina. On April 15 two hundred students from ten states attended a conference in which King was the keynote speaker. Although King believed it was best for the new organization to be independent of SCLC, he was pleased some students carried signs that read "Remember the teachings of Gandhi and Martin Luther King." The conference gave birth to the Student Nonviolent Coordinating Committee (SNCC), which became a powerful force against racism.

Freedom Riders

Like the Montgomery boycott, the sit-ins brought new life to civil rights. When James Farmer became head of the Congress of Racial Equality (CORE) in February 1961, he decided to test segregation in interstate travel with Freedom Riders, black and white volunteers who would ride buses into the South to integrate lunch counters, restrooms, and other bus station public facilities.

On May 4 seven black and six white Freedom Riders bought tickets in Washington, D.C., on a Greyhound bus headed for New Orleans, Louisiana. The first arrest came in Charlotte, North Carolina, when Joseph Perkins requested a shoeshine from a white stand. Jailed on a charge of trespassing, Perkins was acquitted the next day and rejoined the Freedom Riders. But the worst was yet to come.

When the bus arrived in Anniston, Alabama, on May 14, members of the Ku Klux Klan (KKK), a white supremacist group, were waiting. Armed with sticks, brass knuckles, and lead pipes, they set fire to the bus and beat riders who fled the burning vehicle. A second group made it to Birmingham the same day and riders were again beaten. On May 20 when a bus reached Montgomery, a large crowd of several hundred attacked the Freedom Riders. Although violence had been expected, police stayed away so whites could beat protesters.

In Atlanta, King was so furious that he went to Montgomery for a mass rally that night in Ralph David Abernathy's First Baptist Church. By the time King arrived, an angry, shouting mob of ten thousand whites ringed the church, but he pushed his way through them.

Freedom Riders watch as smoke billows from their bus after they were attacked by members of the Ku Klux Klan in Anniston, Alabama.

The Freedom Riders huddled inside First Baptist applauded King when he said, "Now is the time to make real the promises of democracy."[66] But they were disappointed when he declined to join them as they continued their journey into Mississippi; he claimed it would violate his probation in Georgia on past civil rights arrests. Said SNCC cofounder John Lewis: "It was a big criticism that he came to the bus station and saw the other people off and he refused to go."[67]

National Guard soldiers dispatched by President John F. Kennedy were on the bus to protect Freedom Riders. But when it arrived in Jackson, Mississippi, protesters were arrested on various charges and sent to jail. That summer hundreds of Freedom Riders traveled south and were arrested and beaten. On November 1 the Interstate Commerce Commission rewarded their courage by outlawing segregation in interstate bus facilities.

King Fights Too

Although King was only indirectly involved in the daring new initiatives, he had made them possible by his own battles against racism. King would continue to fight in his own way, chiefly through SCLC, which under his leadership grew from a staff of five people and a budget of sixty-three thousand dollars in 1960 to forty workers and a budget of eight hundred thousand dollars in 1963. SCLC concentrated on voter registration and training protesters, including many who took part in sit-ins and Freedom Rides, to use nonviolent tactics.

King, however, was always willing to help the cause of civil rights in any way he could. In late 1961 King received an invitation he could not refuse. It resulted in a trip to Albany, Georgia, where he would suffer his first defeat.

The Albany Movement

Blacks in Albany had been marching to integrate public facilities and being arrested since September. The fight was started by SNCC, and gradually other organizations joined to form a coalition known as the Albany Movement. The group was headed by Dr. William E. Anderson, a black osteopath.

Because the movement had failed to win concessions from city officials, Anderson in December invited King to Albany in hopes that he would strengthen their fight. On December 15 at Shiloh Baptist Church, King told people at a mass rally to continue fighting: "Keep moving. Walk together children, don't you get weary. There's a great camp meeting [spiritual gathering] in the sky."[68] The next day King and Abernathy marched with protesters to city hall and were among 275 people arrested for parading without a permit.

King vowed to remain in jail until the city integrated public facilities. After several days, however, King and Abernathy posted bail because King

A police officer arrests Martin Luther King in Albany, Georgia. King's arrest in Albany led to his first defeat in his campaign for civil rights.

believed city officials and protesters had agreed to negotiate their differences. But after King left jail, nothing happened, because the alleged deal was a nonbinding verbal pact. King had been tricked by white officials, and his decision to leave jail weakened the protests. King felt so bad that he apologized to Albany blacks:

I'm sorry I was bailed out. I didn't understand at the time what was happening. We thought the victory had been won. When we got out, we discovered it was all a hoax.[69]

King vowed to help Albany win. In the next year he repeatedly returned to lead protests and was jailed twice more. But Albany blacks became so embittered by the lack of progress that on the night of July 24, 1962, two thousand blacks rioted, battling police with rocks and bottles. Leaders from various groups involved also began fighting over who was in control, further weakening the effort.

By August 1962 King decided to leave Albany. Although King had suffered a bitter defeat, he was not giving up. He would choose his next battlefield more carefully. It would be Birmingham, Alabama, a city of 350,000 including 140,000 blacks.

Getting Ready

During the Montgomery boycott, the Reverend Fred Shuttlesworth had often driven one hundred miles from Birmingham because he was excited about what King was doing; Shuttlesworth even organized his own boycott in 1956. On January 10, 1963, King and Shuttlesworth met to discuss

fighting segregation in Birmingham, a city Shuttlesworth claimed had "a heart as hard as the steel it manufactures and as black as the coal it mines."[70]

Birmingham's police force and white citizens had always used violence against blacks who sought integration. Even though Shuttlesworth had been beaten with brass knuckles and chains and his wife stabbed when she tried to enroll black children in a white school, he was not afraid to fight: "We mean to kill segregation or be killed by it."[71]

Martin Luther King is arrested in Birmingham, Alabama, for leading an antisegregation march. During his time in prison, King drafted his famous "Letter From A Birmingham Jail."

Despite the threat of violence, King believed he could win in Birmingham after having lost in Albany, because there would be no bickering with other groups about who was in charge. He also admired Shuttlesworth and knew they could work together.

SCLC began planning strategy, and King helped raise $475,000 to bail out arrested demonstrators and fund other activities. In early April, King issued the "Birmingham Manifesto." It explained the problems blacks faced, called for integration of downtown lunch counters, water fountains, and restrooms, and sought to end a ban on black workers in downtown businesses and local government.

Shuttlesworth began the protests on April 3 by leading fifty-two people into five white-only stores; twenty demonstrators were arrested. Despite their reputation for mistreating blacks, police did not act violently and the protests were peaceful.

King Writes a Letter

By April 10 some three hundred protesters had been jailed. The city won an injunction barring King and other leaders from taking part in more protests, but on April 12, Good Friday, King marched anyway. King was arrested and placed in solitary confinement. King remained in jail for over a week—unlike in Albany, he did not post bail right away—and in his cell he wrote "Letter From A Birmingham Jail." In the letter King defended the right of blacks to fight for their rights:

We know through painful experience that freedom is never voluntarily given by the oppressor; it must be demanded by the oppressed. For years now I have heard the word "Wait!" It rings in the ear of every Negro with piercing familiarity. This "Wait" has almost always meant "Never." . . . Oppressed people cannot remain oppressed forever. The yearning for freedom eventually manifests itself, and that is what has happened to the American Negro.[72]

Visitors smuggled King's dramatic, passionate letter out of jail page by page. Newspapers and magazines around the world printed it, creating sympathy for protesters and making them bolder. After King was released April 20, he and Shuttlesworth decided larger marches were necessary. And to make them more dramatic, they agreed that younger people, whose futures were also at stake, should take part.

On May 2 a small army of young people began walking downtown in small groups. "Get those little niggers,"[73] bellowed a furious Eugene "Bull" Connor, Birmingham's police chief, and 959 youths ranging in age from six to sixteen were arrested. The next day young people marched again. This time violence would erupt to give rise to the nickname "Bloody Birmingham."

Training Protesters

All of the men, women, and children who took part in civil rights protests knew that they faced danger from violence by police or white bystanders. To minimize the harm these people might encounter, the Southern Christian Leadership Conference held training sessions for demonstrators so they would know how to act during the events and especially when they were arrested. In And the Walls Came Tumbling Down: Ralph David Abernathy An Autobiography, *Abernathy explains the instructions given to demonstrators:*

We showed them how to march along bent over, elbows guarding their stomachs and hands covering their eyes and temples. We devised this technique for use in the event that we were bombarded with flying rocks and bottles while demonstrating. We also taught a modified version of the same maneuver for use while being beaten with fists or billy clubs. Then, too, we told everyone to go limp when anyone laid hands on them during an arrest. In the first place, it signaled to the arresting officer that he would encounter no active resistance; hence there was no need for excessive force. But equally important, a limp body was harder to handle, took more time to haul into a paddywagon, and therefore limited the efficiency of the police. In fact, over the years, this technique probably saved us enormous sums of money since it reduced signifi-cantly the number of bail bonds we had to pay [to free arrested protesters from jail].

Three civil rights protesters hold hands and brace themselves against the blast of a high-pressure fire hose.

Blood in the Streets

Connor now turned ugly, ordering the use of attack dogs and high-pressure fire hoses to disperse young marchers. "I want to see the dogs work," shouted Connor, who later gleefully commented, "Look at those niggers run."[74] Added to the gruesome images of snarling dogs and powerful jets of water that swept children off their feet were club-wielding policemen, who rained blows upon defenseless protesters.

Although the violence upset King, he had realized it was a possibility. He also knew that the bloody scenes would shock and anger people around the world when they were replayed on television. Among those sickened by them was President John F. Kennedy, who in a quote that echoed King's letter from jail admitted that he could now "well understand why the Negroes of Birmingham are tired of being asked to be patient [for equal rights]."[75]

The police violence continued the next few days; on May 7 Shuttlesworth was slammed into a building so hard by a jet of water that he was knocked unconscious. But King's strategy of using many protesters, as many as twenty-five hundred in a single day, enabled them to slip by Connor's barricades, dogs, and hoses and for the first time to reach the downtown, where they appalled whites by singing "We Shall Overcome" and other civil rights songs.

The bravery of the marchers made business and political leaders realize the protesters were not going to surrender. The two sides began negotiating, and on May 10 King announced an agreement that he claimed would make Birmingham an example to the world of progressive race relations. Officials promised that in the next ninety days they would desegregate public facilities and begin hiring some black workers.

It was a huge victory for King, cementing his role as the nation's preeminent civil rights leader. But the triumph was once again met by white violence. On May 11 racists bombed several Birmingham buildings including the home of King's brother, A.D., and the Gaston Motel, headquarters for SCLC workers. Black residents met white violence with their own, throwing rocks and setting fires in white businesses.

President Kennedy had to dispatch federal troops to restore order to embattled Birmingham. The white backlash, however, was not over. Violence continued there sporadically for months. On September 15 a bomb detonated at a church, killing four young girls in one of the most brutal terrorist acts in the entire civil rights battle. That incident earned the city the title "Bombingham."

King and Kennedy

The president's intervention was only one of many events that linked Kennedy and King. But although Kennedy helped blacks, King always believed he should have done more. In

Governor George Wallace stands in front of the University of Alabama to bar the entrance of James Hood and Vivian Malone. Only after President Kennedy sent National Guard troops to the school did Wallace allow the black students to enroll.

early 1961 King asked Kennedy to create a cabinet level secretary of integration for race relations. Kennedy not only declined but told King that blacks should move more slowly in seeking their rights to avoid a punishing white backlash. "The administration," King would claim, "often retreats from a [civil rights] battlefield which it has proclaimed a field of honor."[76]

The Birmingham violence as well as King's personal pleas helped force Kennedy and his brother, Attorney General Robert F. Kennedy, to start using the power of the federal government to actively ensure black rights. On June 11 Kennedy sent the National Guard to the University of Alabama to enforce a court order allowing James Hood and Vivian Malone to enroll there. That night in a nationally televised speech, Kennedy explained his action and backed civil rights more strongly and passionately than any president ever had:

> We are confronted primarily with a moral issue. It is as old as the scriptures and is as clear as the American Constitution. The heart of the question is whether all Americans are to be afforded equal rights and equal opportunities, whether we are going to treat our fellow Americans as we want to be treated.[77]

On June 19 the president introduced a civil rights bill to back up his dramatic words; it outlawed segrega-tion in interstate public accommodations, empowered the government to aggressively enforce school integration, and banned federal funds to programs that practiced discrimination. Three days later Kennedy met with King and other black leaders about a march they were planning in the nation's capital on August 28. Kennedy was worried the event could hurt support for civil rights if it erupted into violence, but he gave his consent. The event would mark the high point of King's life.

March on Washington

The Prayer Pilgrimage in 1957 had been an emotional and important event for King, but it paled in comparison to the August 28 March on Washington, which attracted 250,000 people. The largest civil rights gathering in the nation's history electrified the world with the passion and power displayed by whites and blacks who came together to support equality for people of all races.

There were many speakers that day, but the one history remembers was King. In his "I Have A Dream" speech, King spoke more eloquently about the need for justice for blacks than anyone ever had. King's words were all the more poignant because they were spoken in the shadow of the monument honoring President Abraham Lincoln, who exactly one hundred years earlier during the Civil War had issued the Emancipation Proclamation to give blacks their freedom.

King Has a Dream

The following are excerpts from "I Have A Dream," the speech Martin Luther King Jr. gave August 28, 1963, in the March on Washington. The transcript is from the Creighton University web site (www.creighton.edu):

Five score years ago, a great American, in whose symbolic shadow we stand signed the Emancipation Proclamation. This momentous decree came as a great beacon light of hope to millions of Negro slaves who had been seared in the flames of withering injustice. It came as a joyous daybreak to end the long night of captivity.... [But] One hundred years later, the life of the Negro is still sadly crippled by the manacles of segregation and the chains of discrimination. One hundred years later, the Negro lives on a lonely island of poverty in the midst of a vast ocean of material prosperity. One hundred years later, the Negro is still languishing in the corners of American society and finds himself an exile in his own land. So we have come here today to dramatize an appalling condition. In a sense we have come to our nation's capital to cash a check. When the architects of our republic wrote the magnificent words of the Constitution and the Declaration of Independence, they were signing a promissory note to which every American was to fall heir. This note was a promise that all men would be guaranteed the inalienable rights of life, liberty, and the pursuit of happiness. It is obvious today that America has defaulted on this promissory note insofar as her citizens of color are concerned. . . . Now is the time to rise from the dark and

King began by noting that a century after Lincoln had abolished slavery "the Negro is still not free" because of racism. He then spoke directly from his heart to people around the world of a simple vision of the future he had:

I have a dream that one day this nation will rise up and live out the true meaning of its creed: "We hold these truths to be self-evident: that all men are created equal." . . . I have a dream that my four children will one day live in a nation where they will not be judged by the color of their skin but by the content of their character.[78]

A Violent Future

After leaving the stage to a thunderous ovation, King, Asa P. Randolph, and other black leaders met privately with Kennedy. The president congratulated desolate valley of segregation to the sunlit path of racial justice. Now is the time to open the doors of opportunity to all of God's children. Now is the time to lift our nation from the quicksands of racial injustice to the solid rock of brotherhood. . . . There will be neither rest nor tranquillity in America until the Negro is granted his citizenship rights. The whirlwinds of revolt will continue to shake the foundations of our nation until the bright day of justice emerges. . . . The marvelous new militancy which has engulfed the Negro community must not lead us to distrust of all white people, for many of our white brothers, as evidenced by their presence here today, have come to realize that their destiny is tied up with our destiny and their freedom is inextricably bound to our freedom. We cannot walk alone.

Martin Luther King gestures toward the crowd during his "I Have A Dream" speech in August 1963.

King on the power of his speech, and everyone was elated over the success of the event, which many historians believe marked the pinnacle of the entire Civil Rights movement.

Yet just a few months after joyously greeting the triumphant King, Kennedy would be assassinated on November 22 in Dallas, Texas. King claimed the president's death could be attributed to the moral climate in America, which allowed people "to express their disagreement through violence," as white racists had done in opposing integration in Birmingham. "We have created an atmosphere," King said, "in which violence and hatred have become popular pastimes."[79]

In the next few years King, more than ever before, would have to battle those forces as he continued to fight for civil rights.

Chapter Five

NEW CHALLENGES, NEW VICTORIES

The dramatic victory in Birmingham, Alabama, and his inspiring speech in the March on Washington vaulted Martin Luther King Jr. to new heights of fame, glory, and respect. *Time* magazine named King its "Man of the Year" for 1963, dubbing him "the symbol of the revolution"[80] in race relations, which dominated headlines that year and which King, more than any single person, had created and led. In December 1964 King gained an even greater honor—the Nobel Peace Prize. At age thirty-five King was the youngest recipient, the second American, and only the third black to receive the prestigious award given annually to the leader who had done the most to improve the world.

When King accepted it in Oslo, Norway, on December 11, he noted that while blacks had made significant progress in civil rights, "We still have a long, long way to go before the dream of freedom is a reality for the Negro in the United States."[81] Although King said blacks were "no longer afraid" and "shall not be cowed" from demanding their rights, he stressed once again that this fight must continue to be based on nonviolence:

Violence as a way of achieving racial justice is both impractical and immoral. I am not unmindful of the fact that violence often brings about momentary results. Nations have frequently won their independence in battle. But in spite of temporary victories, violence never brings permanent peace. It solves no social problem: it merely creates new and more

Martin Luther King delivers his Nobel Peace Prize acceptance speech in December 1964.

complicated ones. Violence is impractical because it is a descending spiral ending in destruction for all.[82]

King's commitment to nonviolence had led to the Nobel Prize and the reverence in which he was held worldwide.

However, in the same year King was honored for his peaceful tactics, the civil rights battle took a dangerous new turn toward violence, both by whites who opposed equality and by northern blacks angry over the slow pace of progress in improving their lives.

Arrested in Florida

In April and May of 1964 King and other Southern Christian Leadership Conference (SCLC) workers began fighting racism in St. Augustine, Florida, a small tourist town best known as the first permanent European settlement in America. (The Spanish founded it in 1565.) However, the city was a stronghold for the racist Ku Klux Klan (KKK) and infamous for denying blacks their rights.

In 1963 Robert Hayling, a dentist and air force veteran, began trying to desegregate public facilities and register black voters. Klansmen kidnapped him and three others, took them to a deserted area, and beat them with brass knuckles and ax handles. When racists continued to attack blacks, Hayling appealed to King for help, and in spring 1964 King began planning a series of protests there.

King wanted the events to be peaceful. But violence broke out the night of May 28 when Andrew Young of the SCLC was leading a protest march to the city's old Slave Market, where blacks had once been sold. Marchers were met by whites who beat them with bicycle chains and iron pipes. While policemen watched, refusing to protect the blacks, Young was knocked unconscious and many were injured.

Despite the violence King arrived on June 11 to test segregation laws. He made reservations at an exclusive restaurant, but when King and his party showed up, owner James Brock refused to seat them. The two then engaged in the following dialogue:

King: I and my friends have come to lunch.

Brock: We can't serve you. We are not integrated.

King: We'll wait around. We feel you should serve us.

Brock: You can't push this thing. We are a small business. We are caught in the middle of something. We find ourselves between two armed camps [racists and blacks]. If we integrate now it would hurt our business.

King: Can't you see how this humiliates us?[83]

King and his friends were arrested for violating Florida's "unwanted guest law" because they tried to eat at the white restaurant. Jailed for the twelfth time, King was imprisoned for two days before posting nine hundred dollars bail.

Martin Luther King and Reverend Ralph David Abernathy sit in a Florida jail. The two men were arrested in the spring of 1964 for protesting segregation laws in the city of St. Augustine.

A New Civil Rights Bill

The conversation between Brock and King was one type of racism: the polite but still illegal way many whites continued to deny blacks their rights. But the night King was arrested, angry whites displayed a far uglier form of racism when they attacked four hundred peacefully marching blacks. From his jail cell King telephoned President Lyndon B. Johnson, the vice president who had succeeded President John F. Kennedy. Calling the attack a "complete breakdown of law and order,"[84] King demanded that Johnson dispatch federal marshals to restore order.

The president did not send help, and whites continued to attack blacks. The mindless violence, however, backfired on St. Augustine whites. The U.S. Senate was considering the Civil Rights Act of 1964, the bill Kennedy introduced before his death and Johnson had championed since. Grim daily headlines out of Florida convinced more senators the time had come to help blacks, and on June 25 the Senate gave the measure final approval. The strongest civil rights bill ever passed outlawed discrimination in public accommodations, created an Equal Opportunity Commission to end job discrimination, and authorized the U.S. Justice Department to file suits to speed up school integration. Hosea Williams of the SCLC claimed, "The Civil Rights Act was written in Birmingham and passed in St. Augustine."[85]

However, the night the Senate passed the bill, eight hundred Klansmen paraded through St. Augustine, beating blacks with clubs and prompting King to say, "This is the most lawless city I've ever been in. I've never seen this kind of wide-open violence."[86] The violence was born out of the anger whites felt at the thought that they must treat blacks as equals. When violence struck several northern cities just a few weeks later, it arose from a different kind of anger—the rage blacks had because they were not getting equal treatment fast enough.

Black Riots

Blacks in northern cities faced far different conditions from those in the South. Although transportation and most public facilities were integrated, blacks in cities like New York, Boston, and Chicago still faced racism daily. Most urban blacks lived in deteriorating areas called ghettos, attended segregated schools, and faced discrimination in getting decent jobs. As in the South, white policemen often harassed blacks and treated them brutally. It was this last aspect of black life that resulted in the first of the riots that would sweep northern cities in the 1960s.

On July 18 an off-duty white officer killed a fifteen-year-old black in New York City's Harlem area. Angered by what they believed was another example of police brutality, blacks rioted for several days, beating whites and looting and burning stores. Before order was

Why Northern Blacks Were Angry

The riots in northern cities in the summer of 1964 surprised Martin Luther King Jr. But he was quickly able to understand the anger that caused them, which he discussed in the Southern Christian Leadership Conference Newsletter *of July–August 1964. The article below is from* What Manner of Man, *a biography of King by Lerone Bennett Jr.:*

As long as thousands of Negroes in Harlem and all the little Harlems of our nation are hovered up in odorous, rat-infested ghettos; as long as the Negro finds himself smothering in an air-tight cages of poverty in the midst of an affluent society; as long as the Negro feels like an exile in his own land, and sees his plight as a long desolate corridor with no exit sign; as long as he has to attend woefully sub-standard schools and use grossly inadequate recreational facilities; as long as the Negro is daily victimized with dehumanizing squalor and depressing congestion; as long as the Negro finds his flight toward freedom constantly delayed by strong head winds of tokenism and small handouts by the white power structure, there will be an ever-present threat of violence and rioting. It is necessary to be as concerned about getting rid of the environmental conditions that caused the riots as it is to condemn the violence. To deal merely with effects and not with causes will be socially and morally suicidal. Until the Harlems and racial ghettos of our nation are destroyed and the Negro is brought into the mainstream of American life, our beloved nation will be on the verge of being plunged into the abyss of social disruption. No greater tragedy can befall a nation than to leave millions of people with a feeling that they have no stake in their society.

restored, one person was killed, 140 injured, and 500 arrested. Believing King's presence could help calm blacks, New York mayor Robert Wagner invited him to visit. King's trip in late July became a personal disaster because New York blacks believed he was interfering in their problems. Adam Clayton Powell, a Baptist minister and U.S. congressman, complained, "No leader outside Harlem should come into this town and tell us what to do."[87]

King, however, had only been trying to help end the black violence, something he had long been concerned about. "The Negro is shedding himself of his fear," King once said, "and my real worry is how we will keep this fearlessness from rising to violent proportions."[88] His fears came to life again in August as blacks in New Jersey, Illinois, and Pennsylvania allowed their growing anger and frustration over racism to spill over into more riots.

For the next few years similar disturbances would break out sporadically in big cities. Although the riots upset King, he was more concerned in helping southern blacks gain the political power they needed to free them from segregation. To do this, they had to be able to vote. It was to secure this right that King went to Selma, Alabama, where fewer than 250 of 15,000 blacks old enough to vote were registered.

Voting Rights

On January 2, 1965, in Selma's Brown Chapel AME Church, King said that winning the right to cast ballots would not be easy. "We must be ready to march," he warned his audience. "We must be ready to go to jail by the thousands. We will bring a voting bill into being on the streets of Selma!"[89]

In January and February a series of marches led to the inevitable arrests of hundreds of protesters including King, who was jailed in February. Those protests sparked similar marches in Marion, Coretta King's hometown. It was there on February 18 that a young black man, Jimmy Lee Jackson, was shot to death by state troopers trying to break up the protest. The death angered blacks so much that a march was planned from Selma to Montgomery to confront Governor George C. Wallace, a staunch segregationist. Although King could not attend, the protest walk was scheduled for March 7.

Bloody Selma

On the day that became known as "Bloody Sunday," five hundred people led by the SCLC's Williams and John Lewis of the Student Nonviolent Coordinating Committee (SNCC) set out from Brown Chapel to the Edmund Pettus Bridge. They marched, despite a pledge by Wallace to stop them. At the bridge leading out of town, they were confronted by state troopers and a sheriff's posse.

What happened next would shock millions of Americans when they viewed the brutal scenes on television news programs. After telling the crowd to disperse, but not giving them time to obey the order, state troopers fired tear gas into the crowd, and mounted volunteers rode their horses through and over protesters. Troopers and posse members used clubs, whips, and chains to beat the defenseless men, women, and children. Seventy demonstrators were injured including seventeen who had to be hospitalized in the incident that earned the city the nickname "Bloody Selma."

On March 9 King led fifteen hundred blacks in a second march. But King halted them at the Pettus Bridge, which was guarded heavily by troopers, and walked them back to Brown Chapel. A federal judge had issued an injunction against the march. Unknown to the crowd, King had agreed not to challenge the order after meeting the night before with aides of President

Police officers assault protesters during the Selma march for voting rights. Seventy protesters were injured during the March 7, 1965, attack, which came to be known as "Bloody Sunday."

Johnson, who did not want another violent confrontation. King had meant the walk as a symbolic gesture, but many blacks dubbed it the "Tuesday Turnaround" and claimed he had been afraid to challenge white troopers. "I felt that we had been betrayed," said black marcher Silas Norman.[90]

However, less than two weeks later, on March 21, King led eight thousand white and black protesters out of Selma under the protection of federal troops. On March 25 King joyously marched into Montgomery at the head of twenty-five thousand protesters and led them in a triumphant celebration in Alabama's capital that was viewed with alarm by Governor Wallace and other whites.

Voting Rights Bill

Despite criticism King had received by halting the second walk, the protests he engineered in Selma sparked another important civil rights victory. The reason is that, just as in Birmingham and St. Augustine, the bitter white backlash backfired. Sickened as Kennedy

Violence in Selma

The violence directed at protesters in Selma, Alabama, by white bystanders as well as law enforcement officials, was often frightening. On March 7, 1965, which became known as "Bloody Sunday," one of the marchers who was terrified was eight-year-old Sheyann Webb. Years later when she was in college, Webb wrote of her experience. Her recollections come from The Black Americans: A History in Their Own Words 1619–1983, *edited by Milton Meltzer:*

It seemed like just a few seconds went by and I heard a shout, "Gas! Gas!" And I looked and I saw the troopers charging us again and some of them were swinging their arms and throwing canisters of tear gas. And beyond them I saw the horsemen starting their charge toward us. I was terrified. I saw those horsemen coming toward me and they had those awful masks on. They rode right through the cloud of tear gas. Some of them had clubs, others had rods or whips, which they swung about them like they were driving cattle. I just turned and ran. And just as I was turning the tear gas got me; it burned my nose first and then got my eyes. I was blinded by the tears. So I began running and not seeing where I was going. People were running and falling and ducking and you could hear the horses' hooves on the pavement and you'd hear people scream and hear the whips swishing and you'd hear them striking the people.

They'd cry out; some moaned. Women as well as men were getting hit. I never got hit, but one of the horses went right by me and I heard the swish sound as the whip went over my head and cracked some man across the back. All of a sudden somebody was grabbing me under the arms and lifting me up and running. And I looked up and saw it was Hosea Williams [of the Southern Christian Leadership Conference] who had me and he was running.

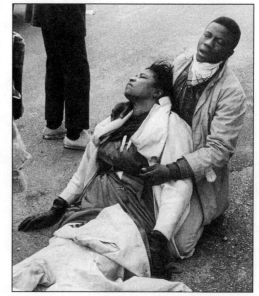

A man cradles a fellow protester injured during the "Bloody Sunday" attack in Selma, Alabama.

had been over similar scenes of police violence in Birmingham, President Johnson claimed what happened in Selma "was an American tragedy."[91] And Johnson, who in January had refused King's request for such legislation, said he would propose a voting rights bill.

The blood that was spilled in Selma led to the 1965 Voting Rights Act, which authorized federal intervention to ensure blacks could vote. Johnson signed it into law on August 6. King was delighted. He knew that in the years to come the bill would enable southern blacks, who often held a voting majority, to elect black mayors, sheriffs, legislators, and governors. This ballot power would do more than anything else to make their lives better.

Having won the voting battle in the South, King turned his attention to the problems of blacks outside the South. The need to do this was dramatically driven home to King just five days after the Voting Rights Act became law, when a riot erupted on August 11 in Watts, the black ghetto in Los Angeles, California. Before it ended on August 16, thirty-five people including twenty-eight blacks had been killed; there was also hundreds of millions of dollars in property damage, leaving much of the area a burned-out wasteland.

As his first northern battleground King chose Chicago, Illinois, a city hit by rioting just two days after Watts erupted. But like Albany, Georgia, it would be the site for one of his rare defeats.

King Goes to Chicago

Except for brief forays into northern cities to speak or lead protest marches, King had concentrated his civil rights efforts in the South. But on January 22, 1966, Martin and Coretta moved into a run-down apartment on Chicago's West Side. Their goal was to spotlight the terrible conditions in which many blacks lived. The Reverend Ralph David Abernathy, who had been at King's side since Montgomery, said the apartment buildings reminded him of bombed-out structures he had seen in Europe after World War II:

> Windows [were] broken out and [there were] mounds of rubble instead of yards. And the odor was unbearable. It was a little like a city dump, except that along with the garbage you constantly smelled human waste. There was no stopping it.[92]

King believed the tactics of nonviolence that triumphed in the South could win in the North. Although he would not stay in Chicago full time, over the next nine months King led marches into white areas to protest segregated housing and education, spoke at scores of rallies, and tried to convince local leaders like Mayor Richard J. Daley to help blacks.

Martin Luther King takes cover after being hit by a rock during a march in Chicago. Although King concentrated his efforts in the South, he did speak out against the appalling living conditions of northern blacks.

Believing that segregated housing was the biggest problem, King in late July began marching into white neighborhoods to build support for open housing legislation to enable blacks to live where they wanted; many whites refused to sell or rent homes and apartments to blacks. But marchers ran into angry whites who hurled bricks and stones, called blacks "monkeys," and chanted "Kill 'em! White Power!" leading King to comment after one ugly incident on August 5 that "I have never seen so much hatred and hostility on the faces of so many people as I've seen here today."[93] King was struck in the head by a rock that very night.

But black violence also erupted. A riot broke out on July 12 when blacks began fighting with police who were turning off fire hydrants they had opened to cool themselves off on a one hundred-degree

King Made a Mistake in Choosing Chicago

From the time Martin Luther King Jr. became a civil rights leader by leading the bus boycott in Montgomery, Alabama, the Reverend Ralph David Abernathy had been one of his most trusted friends. While shouldering much of the responsibility for operation of the Southern Christian Leadership Conference, the Baptist minister was also one of King's most trusted advisers. Abernathy freely admits that King was wrong to choose Chicago, Illinois, in his campaign to bring the battle for civil rights to northern blacks. In And the Walls Came Tumbling Down: Ralph David Abernathy An Autobiography, *Abernathy explains that neither he nor King really understood the problems in Chicago and that they were too big a challenge for them:*

We should have known better than to believe we could come to Chicago and right its wrongs with the same tactics we had used in Montgomery, Birmingham, and Selma. We entered a different world, a world we didn't fully understand. While in some respects [life there] was much better than the South, in some ways it was much worse; and before we had fully understood the differences between the two social views, we had suffered our first significant defeat since Albany. It was an embittering experience, and I'm not sure Martin ever got over it. Perhaps the most important difference we encountered in Chicago was the sheer size of the city. [After a tour of Chicago] I recall looking over at Martin and both of us shaking our heads. The number of people living in squalid deprivation was beyond our comprehension. We were used to dealing with constituencies that numbered in the thousands. Here we could be dealing on behalf of hundreds of thousands.

day. Although illegal, it was a common practice in black areas, which lacked swimming pools that people enjoyed in white neighborhoods. The confrontation escalated into several days of looting and violence in which 2 blacks were killed, 5 injured, and 282 arrested. Several riots broke out in other cities, a common chain reaction in the turbulent 1960s.

King Fails

Despite his efforts King failed to rally substantial numbers of blacks to his cause. Although the black community

---

King Speaks in Montgomery

When the footsore and weary marchers finally reached Montgomery, Alabama, they gathered on the grounds of the Alabama capitol to celebrate. Biographer David Levering Lewis claims the speech Martin Luther King Jr. gave that day was one of his best. The following passages are from Levering's King: A Biography:

Last Sunday more than eight thousand of us started on a mighty walk from Selma, Alabama. We have walked on meandering highways and rested our bodies on rocky byways. I can say as Sister Pollard said [during the Montgomery bus boycott]. One day she was asked while walking if she didn't want a ride, and when she answered "No," the person said, "Well, aren't you tired?" and with ungrammatical [wisdom], she said, "My feets is tired, but my soul is rested." They told us we wouldn't get here. And there were those who said that we could get here only over their dead bodies, but all the world together knows that we are here and that we are standing before the forces of power in the state of Alabama, saying, "We ain't gonna' let nobody turn us around."

King then told the happy crowd that blacks were finally beginning to win their fight for civil rights and that victory was at hand:

My people, my people, listen! The battle is in our hands. I know some of you are asking today, "How long will it take?" I come to say to you this afternoon however difficult the moment, however frustrating the hour, it will not be long, because truth pressed to earth will rise again.

How long? Not long, because no lie can live forever.

How Long? Not long, because you will reap what you sow.

How long? Not long, because the arm of the moral universe is long but it bends toward justice.

was huge—nearly a third of the city's population of 3.5 million—and included many influential civil rights, civic, and social groups, they never united behind King as southern blacks had. One reason is that there was no single issue, such as segregated busing, to bring them together. Instead the issues in Chicago were far more complex, caused as much by the economic poverty that gripped blacks as by racism.

As a result of this the Chicago movement was never as powerful as King had hoped. In the end King was only able to persuade Daley and other Chicago officials on August 26 to sign a ten-point "Summit Agreement" in which they promised to address problems such as segregated housing and schools. But it would prove to be only a paper victory for King. The pact would do almost nothing to change conditions for blacks because officials ignored it. At a rally before leaving Chicago, King was uncharacteristically pessimistic. "Morally, we ought to have what we say in the slogan Freedom Now. But it all doesn't come now. That's a sad fact of life you have to live with,"[94] he admitted.

Another fact of life King had to contend with every day was the enmity of one of the nation's most powerful officials—J. Edgar Hoover. In 1966, and for many years before then, the dictatorial head of the Federal Bureau of Investigation (FBI) had been trying to destroy King's reputation.

J. Edgar Hoover (pictured) and the FBI closely monitored the movements and correspondence of Martin Luther King.

J. Edgar Hoover

As early as 1957 Hoover, who ruled the FBI with an iron hand for a half-century, ordered FBI agents to monitor King's activities. Much of this surveillance was illegal: telephone wiretaps, secret recordings from microphones placed in King's office and hotel rooms, and break-ins to seize written information. Hoover did this because he was afraid King's fight for civil rights would create social unrest. After his 1963 speech at the March on Washington, Hoover claimed King was "the most dangerous Negro [to] the future of this nation."[95]

One of Hoover's concerns was that one of King's white advisers, Stanley Levison, had been affiliated with the Communist Party decades earlier. Although King opposed communism, Hoover believed his association with Levison proved King was a Communist, something the FBI chief was never able to prove.

Hoover was also angry that King began criticizing the FBI in 1961 for not doing enough to protect blacks from white violence in Albany. King claimed this happened because FBI agents in the South were closely allied with local law enforcement officials, who were themselves often racists, or were themselves southerners with antiblack attitudes.

King's Private Life

When Hoover disliked people, he probed their private lives in hopes of catching them doing something immoral or embarrassing; he then used this information to force them to do what he wanted. In investigating King, Hoover discovered that the Baptist minister, married and with four children, frequently had sex with many women. Hoover even made audio recordings of King's dates with women and sent a copy to Coretta.

In his efforts to weaken King, Hoover tried to use the news media to destroy his reputation. Hoover would drop hints to reporters about King's alleged Communist connections and his womanizing. Hoover was especially furious when King won the Nobel Prize. Before King went to Norway to accept the award, Hoover on November 18, 1964, told a group of women reporters to attack King because he was "the most notorious liar in the country" and "one of the lowest characters in America."[96] Because Hoover did not back up his allegations with facts, no stories were written.

Although Hoover was correct that King's secret sex life was immoral, details of his affairs were not publicized until after his death. King himself realized they were wrong, but he also knew that even good men sometimes did bad things.

In his sermons, King often alluded to the split natures many people have: "Within the best of us there is some evil, and within the worst of us there is some good."[97] Most historians believe Hoover displayed a similar duality of nature through his illegal monitoring of public figures like King, who despite this weakness did so much to help make America a better place to live.

Chapter Six

THE DREAM DIES

Martin Luther King Jr.'s failure to achieve meaningful reform in Chicago, Illinois, ignited a tidal wave of criticism. Black leaders there like Chester Robinson called the paper promises "a sell out" and claimed "this agreement is a lot of words that give us nothing specific we can understand."[98] Nationally what was considered a personal defeat for King accelerated a growing disillusionment among blacks about his tactics of nonviolence, which many now believed were no longer strong enough to achieve positive results.

But even though King had been the most influential civil rights leader for a decade, criticism of him was nothing new. Some blacks had always rejected King's reliance on nonviolence, mainly because white racists used violence to keep them in submission, and others had believed he was too passive, sometimes even timid, in pursuit of racial justice. As early as 1962 Louis E. Lomax wrote in *The Negro Revolt* that some sit-in protesters and Freedom Riders believed the latter:

> The honeymoon between Dr. King and others close to the Negro Revolt is over; for the first time since Montgomery criticism of Dr. King is now appearing in print, and comes from, of all people, the Negro students. His crime seems to be that he has not gone to jail enough to merit the badge of continuing leadership. Students are not only idealistic, they are impatient.[99]

Although such criticism hurt King, it also made him reconsider his thinking about how to help blacks achieve equality. And to the surprise of many, King's personal philosophy on the Civil Rights movement began to change.

King's Critics

One of King's harshest critics was Malcolm X, who was born Malcolm Little but changed his name when he became a Muslim. He claimed "Little" was a slave name given to his family by whites who once owned them. Malcolm believed blacks should defend themselves against white violence, with guns if necessary. In a slap at King, Malcolm once said, "Any Negro who teaches other Negroes to turn the other cheek is disarming the Negro of his moral right, of his natural right, of his intelligent right to defend himself."[100]

Malcolm influenced many blacks as a spokesman for the Nation of Islam, a group known as the Black Muslims that preached blacks could not trust whites and should live separately from them. Although King believed blacks and whites had to learn to live together in harmony, he agreed with Malcolm that blacks needed to have more pride in themselves and their heritage.

Two other groups that attacked King were the Student Nonviolent Coordinating Committee (SNCC), which King had helped start, and the Congress of Racial Equality (CORE). In the mid-1960s, both organizations began to stress the concept of "Black Power" and to abandon the nonvio-

lence that was the core of King's philosophy.

Black Power

In 1966 new SNCC chairman Stokely Carmichael began advocating militant tactics, including retaliation against racists who used violence against blacks. Carmichael also wanted to exclude whites, whom King considered valuable allies, from the Civil Rights movement because he believed blacks should win the battle themselves; he even began using the word "honky," a derisive term for whites. This new philosophy was summed up in the term "Black Power," which Carmichael explained in an August 5, 1966, article in the *New York Times*:

> The only way we gonna stop them white men from whuppin' us is to take over. We been saying freedom for six years [since the sit-ins began] and we ain't got nothin'. What we gonna start saying now is Black Power![101]

Carmichael first used the phrase on June 4, 1966, in Greenwood, Mississippi, where SNCC was trying to register voters, and it was not long before King was confronted with this new philosophy. On June 6 James Meredith, the first black student at the University of Mississippi, was shot while marching from Memphis, Tennessee, to Jackson, Mississippi, to

Stokely Carmichael speaks at a civil rights gathering. Carmichael and King disagreed on the role whites should play in the Civil Rights movement.

prove blacks could travel freely and without fear in the South.

When Meredith was wounded, King met with Carmichael and CORE's Floyd McKissick to discuss finishing Meredith's march. King quickly became upset by their Black Power stance. "I'm not going to beg the white man for anything I deserve," Carmichael belligerently told King. "I'm going to take it."[102]

Fearing that the march could turn violent, King convinced SNCC, CORE, and other black groups to keep the event peaceful. But the protest in June was marred by violence when whites in Canton and Philadelphia, both in Mississippi, attacked marchers; police intervened only when blacks began fighting back. At rallies along the way, Carmichael's shouts of "Black Power" were joyously received, while King's gentler message was sometimes booed.

When the march ended, King was upset at the new direction for the Civil Rights movement. "What is needed," King said, "is a strategy for change. A tactical program that will bring the Negro into the mainstream of American life as quickly as possible."[103]

But before King could conceive such a new program, he would have to change his own thinking.

King's Philosophy Shifts

In late 1966 King was disappointed not only over Chicago but another series of black riots that had swept through more than forty cities, including his hometown of Atlanta, Georgia, and midwestern Milwaukee, Wisconsin. The riots were fueled by the anger blacks felt that they were still being denied their rights, a bitterness King himself displayed during the Chicago protests when he declared, "I'm tired of marching for something that should have been mine at birth."[104]

However, it was not just anger that King shared with other blacks. Even though King often disagreed with the tactics and rhetoric of leaders like Carmichael and Malcolm X—King opposed the term "Black Power" because he said it could be interpreted as an "unconscious and often conscious call for retaliatory violence"[105]—he held many of the same beliefs they did. In *My Life with Martin Luther King, Jr.*, Coretta Scott King wrote:

> He shared [with Malcolm X] the fierce desire that the black American reclaim his racial pride, his joy in himself and his race in a physical, a cultural, and a spiritual rebirth. He shared the sure knowledge that "black is beautiful" [and] Martin also believed in Black Power. He believed that we must have our share of the economy, of education, of jobs, of free choice.[106]

King slowly began to reassess the direction of the Civil Rights movement and his own beliefs. King biographer Michael Eric Dyson believes events in Chicago as well as those in Mississippi and other places in 1966 irrevocably reshaped King's thinking. Explains Dyson:

> It is clear that when it comes to dating the evolution of King's political philosophy, "B.C." must refer to "Before Chicago," before his encounter with persistent poverty, and "A.D." must mean "After Defeat," not simply of his programs in Chicago, but of his faith in American liberal reform to respond adequately to the needs of blacks and the poor.[107]

His new understanding of American society led him to the disheartening conclusion that the victories he helped engineer had failed to give southern blacks their full rights—white officials still kept many from voting, and racist groups like the Ku Klux Klan used violence to intimidate those who kept battling for their rights—and had done little to improve life for northern blacks. Although King realized that individual racism was at the core of the

Martin and Malcolm

Although Martin Luther King Jr. and Malcolm X often disagreed on philosophy and tactics that should be used in the battle for civil rights, the two black leaders respected each other. In To Make the Wounded Whole: The Cultural Legacy of Martin Luther King, Jr., *author Lewis V. Baldwin writes that by early 1965 the two were growing closer together in thought about the fight for black rights:*

One of the best indications of the growing unity between Malcolm and King occurred during SCLC's [Southern Christian Leadership Conference's] Selma campaign in early February 1965, some three weeks before Malcolm's death. Malcolm visited Selma while the movement was in full swing, addressed the SCLC and an enthusiastic crowd of Student Nonviolent Coordinating Committee (SNCC) supporters at the Brown Chapel A.M.E, and spoke personally with Coretta Scott King about his desire "to work with Dr. King and not against him." King was confined in a Selma jail at the time. "I want Dr. King to know that I didn't come to Selma to make his job difficult," Malcolm explained to Coretta Scott King. "I really did come thinking that I could make it easier. If the white people realize what the alterna-tive [to King] is, perhaps they will be more willing to hear Dr. King." Both King and his wife were impressed and moved by Malcolm's sincerity on that occasion but were convinced [King later wrote] that he was not yet able to renounce violence and overcome the bitterness which life had invested to him. Even so, the spirit and atti-tude Malcolm reflected in Selma made King more receptive to the possibility of meeting with him. [Before the meeting could take place, Malcolm was assassinated].

Martin Luther King shakes hands with Malcolm X.

problem, he began to believe that poverty was the most powerful factor facing blacks; it wore down their spirits, relegated them to dismal housing, and denied them any opportunity to improve their lives. King began to believe that deeper changes than simply a few laws were needed so blacks could achieve true equality. In the summer of 1967 King admitted:

> For years I labored with the idea of reforming the existing institutions of the society, a little change here, a little change there. Now I feel quite differently. I think you've got to have a reconstruction of the entire society, a revolution of values.[108]

Despite this philosophical transformation, King remained constant to one ideal—he would never surrender his unwavering commitment to nonviolence:

> Even if every Negro in the United States comes to think that Negroes ought to riot [and] if every Negro in the United States turns to violence, I will choose to be that one lone voice preaching that this is the wrong way.[109]

A New Initiative

In the fall of 1967 King unveiled plans to have the Southern Christian Leadership Conference (SCLC) begin a Poor People's Campaign against poverty. And because King knew poverty hurt all people, King decided to also help whites, Hispanics, Native Americans, and anyone else who was poor.

In what King termed an "Economic Bill of Rights," he said the federal government should guarantee people jobs that paid them enough to live decently, end housing discrimination, fund construction of hundreds of thousands of units of low-cost housing, and forcefully pursue school integration; King believed a quality education was the key to poor children being able to escape poverty.

To pressure the federal government to meet his demands, King planned a series of mass demonstrations in Washington, D.C., starting in April 1968. In announcing the protests at Ebeneezer Baptist Church in Atlanta on December 4, 1967, King said that helping the poor was vital to the nation's future. "America," he said, "is at a cross roads of history, and it is critically important for us, as a nation and a society, to choose a new path and move upon it with resolution and courage."[110]

In the past, King had often had the support of powerful white officials like President John F. Kennedy and the sympathy of average whites for the problems blacks faced. But by attacking the nation's economic system, King alienated many white supporters, who now believed his ideas were too radical.

Vietnam

The negative reaction to King's campaign against poverty, however, was small

Martin Luther King and others protest the Vietnam War in 1967. King's antiwar stance was his first criticism of the policies of President Johnson's administration.

compared to the furor that erupted in early 1967 when he opposed the Vietnam War. President Lyndon B. Johnson in the early 1960s had committed hundreds of thousands of soldiers to fight communism in South Vietnam. The war, however, split the nation because many people believed the United States had no just cause to fight there.

In a speech at the Chicago Coliseum on March 25, 1967, King criticized U.S. involvement and called for a negotiated end to the war. Like millions of other Americans, King was horrified that so many innocent civilians were being killed in the fighting. In explaining his opposition on April 4 in New York City, King said,

It would be very inconsistent for me to teach and preach nonviolence and then applaud violence when thousands and thousands of people, both adults and children, are being maimed and mutilated and many killed in this war, so that I still feel and live by the principle, "Thou shalt not kill."[111]

King's criticism of U.S. officials directing the war effort went against his usual practice of working with elected officials to achieve his goals. Because King had cooperated so often with white officials, blacks like Malcolm X had labeled him an "Uncle Tom," a derisive term comparing him to a slave who obeyed his master's every command. His antiwar stance amounted to open rebellion against the Johnson administration, freeing him from that ugly nickname.

He also opposed the war because he believed it was hurting America by consuming federal dollars needed at home to help poor people. King also realized that most U.S. soldiers fighting and dying in Vietnam were from poor backgrounds, including tens of thousands of blacks. Many poor young men joined the armed forces because they had no other job

A police officer beats a looter during the Memphis, Tennessee, riots of March 1968. Although King came to Memphis to lead the demonstration, he refused to do so when the protest turned violent.

opportunities or could not afford to attend college, which was one way to avoid being drafted to fight in the war.

King participated in many peace rallies in 1967, denouncing what he believed was an unjust war. But in early 1968 battle of a different kind drew him to Memphis, Tennessee—a labor war.

Memphis

On February 1 two black Memphis garbage workers were crushed to death when their truck's automatic compressor was accidentally triggered. The fatal accident was just the latest setback for black and white workers, who had been trying for months to get the city to recognize their union (Local 1733 of the American Federation of State, County, and Municipal Employees), increase their low pay, and improve safety and other working conditions. When the city rejected their demands, workers went on strike on February 12.

King was asked by black ministers to support the dispute. He agreed because it fit in with his Poor People's Campaign, which sought to make sure workers received decent pay. King came to Memphis to lead a protest on March 28, but when he got to the march's starting point, he was alarmed at the behavior of the crowd of over seven thousand people. Some black youths were removing sticks from picket signs, with the obvious intention of using them as clubs, and there were other signs that violence would occur.

"There's violence breaking out, and I can't lead a violent march. Call it off!"[112] King told the Reverend Jim Lawson, a local black minister.

Lawson tried to stop the march, but it was too late; the unruly crowd ignored his commands, issued over a bullhorn, and began heading into the downtown area. As King had foreseen, violence erupted. Blacks angrily broke windows, damaging over 150 stores. They also fought with police, who used tear gas and clubs to subdue protesters and shot one youth to death.

Although the violence had been spearheaded by militant groups like the Invaders and King had tried to stop the march, he was blamed for the riot. The *Memphis Commercial Appeal* wrote that "Dr. King's pose as a leader of a nonviolent movement has been shattered!", a false charge gleefully taken up by whites who had long opposed him. [113]

King Is Shot

To resurrect his reputation, King believed he had to lead a peaceful demonstration, and the second Memphis march was scheduled for April 8. King arrived on April 3 to plan the event and that night spoke at Mason Street Temple. King gave a speech worthy of being long remembered, but his words carried a pessimistic tone. King admitted he might not be alive when blacks fully won their rights, something he had mentioned in some earlier speeches:

Well, I don't know what will happen now. We've got some difficult days ahead, but it really doesn't matter with me now—because I've been to the mountaintop. . . . I may not get there with you. But I want you to know tonight that we, as a people, will get to the Promised Land! And so I'm happy tonight! I'm not fearing any man! Mine eyes have seen the glory of the coming of the Lord![114]

King, Abernathy, and other SCLC workers slept at the Lorraine Motel, King in a second-floor room that had a balcony and faced the parking lot. The next day, April 4, King met with local leaders and SCLC staff about the march. Shortly after 6 P.M., King went out onto his balcony to shout down a reminder to local musician Ben Branch, who was in the parking lot below; he asked Branch to sing "Precious Lord, Take My Hand" at that night's rally.

As King turned back to his room, a loud crack split the air. Shot in the face, King fell to the balcony floor. At the rifle's loud report, Abernathy rushed from King's room and reached down for his friend, who was bleeding heavily from a wound that had torn away the right side of his neck and jaw. Abernathy retrieved a towel from the room and, while cradling King in his arms, he tried to stop the flow of blood from the three-inch wound. King was taken to St. Joseph's Hospital, but

there was nothing doctors could do. King was pronounced dead at 7:05 P.M.

Reaction to King's Death

The assassination was eerily similar to that of President Kennedy five years earlier. The supreme irony was that when Kennedy was shot to death, King had predicted "that's the way I'm going to go."[115] Like that of Kennedy, King's death unleashed a worldwide outpouring of shock and sympathy, with leaders of many countries praising King as a great man.

But at home there was not just shock and sorrow but rage among blacks that their leader had been taken from them. "When white America killed Dr. King, she declared war on us," proclaimed Carmichael, who advised blacks to "get your gun."[116] Sadly, many blacks agreed with Carmichael, and riots flared up in 125 U.S. communities. Before they subsided thirty-nine people, most of them black, had been killed in what *Newsweek* magazine labeled "a black rampage [which was] the most widespread spasm of racial disorder in its violent history."[117] The riots were a tragic, ironic twist to the death of a man devoted to nonviolence.

The blacks who suspected King had been killed by a white racist were correct. He was James Earl Ray, an escaped convict and career criminal. Shortly after the shooting, officials discovered the rifle Ray had fired from

A Witness to King's Death

When Martin Luther King Jr. was shot, the Reverend Ralph David Abernathy rushed out from the hotel room onto the balcony where King lay. Jesse Jackson, who later became a powerful civil rights figure in his own right, claimed that day that he had reached King first and held him while he died. But in And the Walls Came Tumbling Down: Ralph David Abernathy An Autobiography, *Abernathy writes that Jackson was lying: "Yes, I was the last person he spoke to as I was cradling him in my arms." Abernathy describes how he went to King's side as soon as he was shot:*

I bolted out the door and found him there, face up, sprawled and unmoving. Stepping over his [body] I knelt down, gathered him in my arms, and began patting him on his left cheek. Even at the first glance I could see that a bullet had entered his right cheek, leaving a small hole. I looked down at Martin's face. His eyes wobbled, then for an instant focused on me. "Martin. It's all right. Don't worry. This is Ralph. This is Ralph." His eyes grew calm and he moved his lips. I was certain he was trying to say something. Then, in the next instant, I saw the understanding drain from his eyes and leave them absolutely empty. I looked down more carefully at the wound and noticed the glistening blood and a flash of white bone. I felt as if I were on that balcony cradling Martin for hours, but it was actually less than ten minutes from the time the shot rang out until the rescue squad arrived.

Hosea Williams (left), Jesse Jackson, Martin Luther King, and Ralph David Abernathy stand on the balcony of the Lorraine Motel in Memphis the day before King was assassinated.

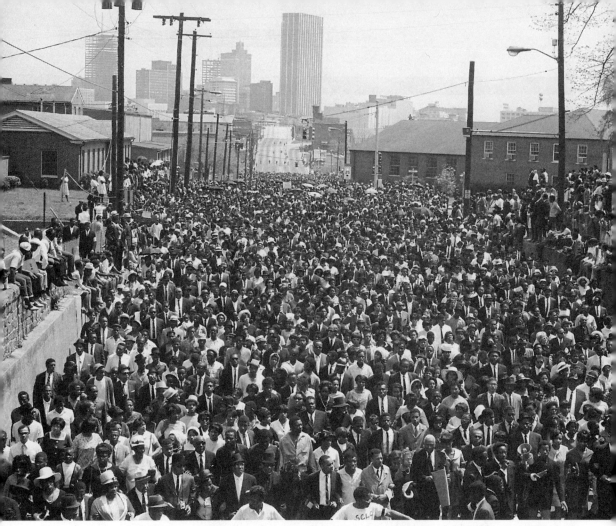

Thousands of mourners participate in a funeral march for Dr. Martin Luther King Jr. on April 9, 1968.

Bessie Brewer's rooming house, just across the street from King's hotel. Authorities quickly identified Ray and tracked him to London, England, where he was arrested on June 8. Ray entered a guilty plea on March 9, 1969, to a charge of murder and was sentenced to ninety-nine years in prison; he died in prison on April 23, 1998, at age seventy.

When King's funeral was held on April 9 in Ebeneezer Baptist, a grieving Coretta and their four children—Yolanda, Martin Luther III, Dexter Scott, and Bernice Albertine—were the center of attention. The eight hundred guests included powerful officials like Vice President Hubert H. Humphrey, entertainers Harry Belafonte and Sidney Poitier, and Jacqueline Kennedy, the president's widow. Surrounding the church to honor the slain civil rights hero who had done so much for them was a crowd estimated at one hundred thousand.

A Tribute to King

When Martin Luther King Jr. died, tributes to his greatness poured in from around the world from famous people and average men and women. One of the most moving was written by actor Harry Belafonte, a close friend and comrade in the battle for civil rights, and Stanley Levison, one of King's most trusted advisers. The tribute is from My Life with Martin Luther King, Jr., *by Coretta Scott King:*

In a nation tenaciously racist, a black man sensitized its somnolent conscience; in a nation sick with violence, a black man preached nonviolence; in a nation corrosive with alienation, a black man preached love; in a world embroiled in three wars in twenty years, a black man preached peace. When an assassin's bullet ended Martin Luther King's life it failed in its purpose. More people heard his message in four days than in the twelve years of his preaching. His voice was stilled but his message rang clamorously around the globe. He was stoned, stabbed, reviled, and spat upon when he lived, but in death there was a shattering sense that a man of ultimate goodness had lived among us. Martin Luther King died as he lived, fighting to his last breath for justice. In only twelve years of public life he evoked more respect for black people than a preceding century had produced.

A young boy touches the reflecting pool that surrounds Martin Luther King's tomb. King remains an inspiration to many.

In his remarks the Reverend Martin Luther King Sr. claimed, "It was the *hate* in this land that took my son away from me."[118] Although King had fought that same hate all his life, he had never given up hope that his dream of equality would one day come true. His wish for the future is summed up by the words inscribed on his crypt in Atlanta, which are from his March on Washington speech:

FREE AT LAST,
FREE AT LAST
THANK GOD ALMIGHTY
I'M FREE AT LAST[119]

King's Legacy

Today nearly every major American city has a street or school named after King, and since 1986 his country has celebrated his birthday (January 15) with a national holiday on the third Monday of January. But King's true legacy lies not in such personal honors but in the advances in black rights he helped force the nation to accept. Perhaps his final victory came on April 10, when Congress passed the stalled 1968 Civil Rights Bill banning discrimination in housing and

the sale and rental of apartments and homes. Congress acted after President Johnson said its passage was a fitting way to honor King, who had supported the measure.

Some historians believe King's death marked the end of the civil rights drive he helped start. After his slaying, the movement began to weaken. No single leader emerged to replace King, resulting in fighting instead of cooperation between various black groups, and as blacks continued to reject King's philosophy of nonviolence, they lost more and more support from white leaders and citizens.

Biographer Adam Fairclough claims "King's most enduring monument" lies in the rights he helped secure for southern blacks: "The destruction of white supremacy represented an incalculable victory for human freedom."[120]

Although Fairclough maintains that King's "vision and example still inspire and energize" people, he believes King did much more than help blacks: "By confronting America with its most glaring political hypocrisy [Jim Crow laws in a nation dedicated to freedom and equality], he helped to revitalize American democracy."[121]

Notes

Introduction: A Disciple of Nonviolence

1. Quoted in Margaret Truman, *Harry S. Truman*. New York: William Morrow, 1973, p. 52.
2. Lerone Bennett Jr., *What Manner of Man: A Biography of Martin Luther King, Jr.* Chicago: Johnson, 1976, p. 131.
3. Quoted in Marshall Frady, *Martin Luther King, Jr.* New York: Penguin, 2002, p. 5.
4. Louis E. Lomax, *The Negro Revolt*. New York: Harper & Brothers, 1962, p. 82.
5. Martin Luther King Jr.,"I Have A Dream" (speech transcript), August 28, 1963, Creighton University. www.creighton.edu.
6. Martin Luther King Jr., *Stride Toward Freedom: The Montgomery Story*. Reprint. New York: Harper-Collins, 1986, p. 9.

Chapter One: A Preacher's Son

7. Quoted in Michael Eric Dyson, *I May Not Get There with You: The True Martin Luther King, Jr.* New York: Free Press, 2000, p. 307.
8. Quoted in Stephen B. Oates, *The Trumpet Sound: The Life of Martin Luther King, Jr.* New York: Harper & Row, 1982, p. 5.
9. Quoted in Bennett, *What Manner of Man*, p. 18.
10. Quoted in David Levering Lewis, *King: A Biography.* Chicago: University of Illinois Press, 1978. p. 7.
11. Quoted in Frady, *Martin Luther King, Jr.*, p. 15.
12. Quoted in William Roger Witherspoon, *Martin Luther King: To the Mountaintop.* Garden City, NY: Doubleday, 1985, p. 4.
13. Quoted in Witherspoon, *Martin Luther King*, p. 28.
14. Quoted in Oates, *The Trumpet Sound*, p. 17.
15. Quoted in Frady, *Martin Luther King, Jr.*, p. 19.
16. Quoted in Bennett, *What Manner of Man*, p. 29.
17. Quoted in Lewis, *King*, p. 34.
18. King, *Stride Toward Freedom*, pp. 96–97.
19. Quoted in Oates, *The Trumpet Sound*, p. 33.
20. Quoted in Jim Bishop, *The Days of Martin Luther King, Jr.* New York:

G.P. Putnam's Sons, 1971, p. 105.
21. Quoted in Coretta Scott King, *My Life with Martin Luther King, Jr.* New York: Holt, Rinehart and Winston, 1969, p. 52.
22. Quoted in Witherspoon, *Martin Luther King*, p. 15.

Chapter Two: The Montgomery Bus Boycott
23. Quoted in Lewis, *King*, p. 12.
24. Quoted in *Time*, "Martin Luther King Jr.: Never Again Where He Was," January 3, 1964. www.time.com.
25. Quoted in Oates, *The Trumpet Sound*, p. 57.
26. Quoted in Douglas Brinkley, *Rosa Parks*. New York: Penguin Putnam, 2000, p. 107.
27. Quoted in Thomas R. Brooks, *Walls Come Tumbling Down: A History of the Civil Rights Movement 1940–1970*. Englewood Cliffs, NJ: Prentice-Hall, 1974, p. 96.
28. Quoted in Brooks, *Walls Come Tumbling Down*, p. 97.
29. Quoted in Witherspoon, *Martin Luther King*, p. 25.
30. Quoted in Bennett, *What Manner of Man*, p. 64.
31. Quoted in Oates, *The Trumpet Sound*, p. 65.
32. Quoted in Frady, *Martin Luther King, Jr.*, p. 34.
33. Quoted in Frady, *Martin Luther King, Jr.*, p. 35.
34. Quoted in Ralph David Abernathy, *And the Walls Came Tumbling Down: Ralph David Abernathy An Autobiography.* New York: Harper & Row, 1989, p. 154.
35. Quoted in Anthony Lewis, *Portrait of a Decade: The Second American Revolution*. New York: Random House, 1964, p. 17.
36. Quoted in Brinkley, *Rosa Parks*, p. 145.
37. Quoted in Frady, *Martin Luther King, Jr.*, p. 37.
38. Quoted in Witherspoon, *Martin Luther King*, p. 33.
39. King, *Stride Toward Freedom*, p. 135.
40. Quoted in Bennett, *What Manner of Man*, p. 70.
41. Quoted in Bishop, *The Days of Martin Luther King, Jr.*, p. 1.
42. Quoted in Bennett, *What Manner of Man*, p. 77.
43. Quoted in Lewis, *Portrait of a Decade*, p. 78.
44. Quoted in Frady, *Martin Luther King, Jr.*, p. 57.

Chapter Three: King Becomes a National Leader
45. Quoted in Lewis, *Portrait of a Decade*, p. 72.
46. Quoted in Oates, *The Trumpet Sound*, p. 115.
47. Bennett, *What Manner of Man*, p. 79.
48. Quoted in Diane Ravitch, ed., *The American Reader: Words That Moved a Nation*. New York: Harper Perennial, 1991, p. 215.
49. Lewis V. Baldwin, *To Make the*

Wounded Whole: The Cultural Legacy of Martin Luther King, Jr. Minneapolis: Fortress Press, 1992, p. 52.

50. Quoted in Brooks, *Walls Come Tumbling Down*, p. 131.
51. Quoted in Lewis, *King*, p. 93.
52. Quoted in Bennett, *What Manner of Man*, p. 88.
53. Quoted in Brooks, *Walls Come Tumbling Down*, p. 141.
54. Quoted in Frady, *Martin Luther King, Jr.*, p. 57.
55. Quoted in Bishop, *The Days of Martin Luther King, Jr.*, p. 212.
56. King, *Stride Toward Freedom*, p. 196.
57. Quoted in Witherspoon, *Martin Luther King*, p. 61.
58. Quoted in Frady, *Martin Luther King, Jr.*, p. 61.
59. Quoted in Adam Fairclough, *Martin Luther King, Jr.* Athens: University of Georgia Press, 1995, p. 59.
60. Quoted in Frady, *Martin Luther King, Jr.*, p. 76.

Chapter Four: King Pursues His Dream of Racial Justice

61. Quoted in Bennett, *What Manner of Man*, p. 112.
62. Quoted in Brooks, *Walls Come Tumbling Down*, p. 146.
63. Quoted in Lewis, *Portrait of a Decade*, p. 87.
64. Quoted in Bennett, *What Manner of Man*, p. 82.

65. Bennett, *What Manner of Man*, p. 112.
66. Quoted in Witherspoon, *Martin Luther King*, p. 90.
67. Quoted in Frady, *Martin Luther King, Jr.*, p. 74.
68. Quoted in Fairclough, *Martin Luther King, Jr.*, p. 66.
69. Quoted in Frady, *Martin Luther King, Jr.*, p. 91.
70. Quoted in Diane McWhorter, *Carry Me Home: Birmingham, Alabama, The Climactic Battle of the Civil Rights Revolution.* New York: Simon & Schuster, 2001, p. 21.
71. Quoted in McWhorter, *Carry Me Home*, p. 22.
72. Martin Luther King Jr., "Letter From A Birmingham Jail" (letter transcript), Creighton University, www.creighton.edu.
73. Quoted in Witherspoon, *Martin Luther King*, p. 124.
74. Quoted in Frady, *Martin Luther King, Jr.*, p. 113.
75. Quoted in Richard Reeves, *President Kennedy: Profile of Power.* New York: Simon & Schuster, 1993, p. 488.
76. Quoted in Bishop, *The Days of Martin Luther King, Jr.*, p. 248.
77. John F. Kennedy: "Report to the American People on Civil Rights" (speech transcript), June 11, 1963. John Fitzgerald Kennedy Library. www.cs.umb.edu.
78. King, "I Have A Dream"
79. Quoted in Lewis, *King*, p. 236.

Chapter Five: New Challenges, New Victories

80. *Time*, "Martin Luther King Jr.: Never Again Where He Was," January 3, 1964. www.time.com.

81. Martin Luther King Jr., "The Quest for Peace and Justice" (Nobel lecture transcript), December 11, 1964. www.nobel.se

82. King, "The Quest for Peace and Justice."

83. Quoted in Bennett, *What Manner of Man*, p. 202.

84. Quoted in Oates, *The Trumpet Sound*, p. 300.

85. Quoted in Witherspoon, *Martin Luther King*, p. 159.

86. Quoted in Frady, *Martin Luther King, Jr.*, p. 138.

87. Quoted in Thomas R. Brooks, *Walls Come Tumbling Down*, p. 240.

88. Quoted in Abernathy, *And the Walls Came Tumbling Down*, p. 275.

89. Quoted in Frady, *Martin Luther King, Jr.*, p. 154.

90. Quoted in Fred Powledge, *The Civil Rights Movement and the People Who Made It*. Boston: Little, Brown, 1990, p. 625.

91. Quoted in Frady, *Martin Luther King, Jr.*, p. 161.

92. Abernathy, *And the Walls Came Tumbling Down*, p. 370.

93. Quoted in Oates, *The Trumpet Sound*, p. 413.

94. Quoted in Oates, *The Trumpet Sound*, p. 416.

95. Quoted in Curt Gentry, *J. Edgar Hoover: The Man and the Secrets*. New York: W.W. Norton, 1991, p. 528.

96. Quoted in Fairclough, *Martin Luther King, Jr.*, p. 99.

97. Quoted in Frady, *Martin Luther King, Jr.*, p. 65.

Chapter Six: The Dream Dies

98. Quoted in Oates, *The Trumpet Sound*, p. 416.

99. Lomax, *The Negro Revolt*, p. 85.

100. Quoted in Baldwin, *To Make the Wounded Whole*, p. 30.

101. Quoted in William L. Van Deburg, ed., *Modern Black Nationalism: From Marcus Garvey to Louis Farrakhan*. New York: New York University Press, 1997, p. 120.

102. Quoted in Lewis, *King*, p. 322.

103. Quoted in Oates, *The Trumpet Sound*, p. 405.

104. Quoted in Dyson, *I May Not Get There With You*, p. 38.

105. Quoted in Fairclough, *Martin Luther King, Jr.*, p. 116.

106. King, *My Life with Martin Luther King, Jr.*, p. 260.

107. Dyson, *I May Not Get There with You*, p. 84.

108. Quoted in Lewis, *King*, p. 354.

109. Quoted in Frady, *Martin Luther King, Jr.*, p. 184.

110. Quoted in Oates, *The Trumpet*

Sound, p. 451.

111. Quoted in Lewis, *King*.

112. Quoted in Abernathy, *And the Walls Came Tumbling Down*, p. 418.

113. Quoted in Abernathy, *And the Walls Came Tumbling Down*, p. 420.

114. Quoted in Frady, *Martin Luther King, Jr.*, pp. 202–203.

115. Quoted in Bishop, *The Days of Martin Luther King, Jr.*, p. 336.

116. Quoted in Baldwin, *To Make the Wounded Whole*, p. 219.

117. Quoted in Baldwin, *To Make the Wounded Whole*, p. 219.

118. Quoted in Frady, *Martin Luther King, Jr.*, p. 210.

119. Quoted in King, *My Life with Martin Luther King, Jr.*, p. 334.

120. Fairclough, *Martin Luther King, Jr.*, p. 131.

121. Fairclough, *Martin Luther King, Jr.*, p. 131.

FOR FURTHER READING

Jim Bishop, *The Days of Martin Luther King, Jr.* New York: G.P. Putnam's Sons, 1971. A very readable biography of King by a veteran journalist.

Coretta Scott King, *My Life with Martin Luther King, Jr.* New York: Holt, Rinehart and Winston, 1969. King's wife explains her life and her own fight against racism.

Martin Luther King, Jr., *Stride Toward Freedom: The Montgomery Story.* Reprint. New York: HarperCollins, 1986. King documents the bus boycott that launched the modern Civil Rights movement.

Milton Meltzer, ed., *The Black Americans: A History in Their Own Words 1619–1983.* New York: Thomas Y. Crowell, 1984. The historian relies extensively on speeches and writings of past black leaders to tell the story of the black experience in America.

Rosa Parks with Gregory J. Reed, *Quiet Strength: The Faith, the Hope, and the Heart of a Woman Who Changed a Nation.* Grand Rapids, MI: Zondervan, 1994. Parks writes on a number of issues, including her historic part in the Montgomery bus boycott.

Lillie Patterson, *Martin Luther King, Jr. and the Freedom Movement.* New York: Facts On File, 1989. An easy-to-read but thorough biography of King.

ADDITIONAL WORKS CONSULTED

Books

Ralph David Abernathy, *And the Walls Came Tumbling Down: Ralph David Abernathy An Autobiography*. New York: Harper & Row, 1989. King's friend and top aide explains his long civil rights career, which began by helping launch the Montgomery bus boycott.

Lewis V. Baldwin, *To Make the Wounded Whole: The Cultural Legacy of Martin Luther King, Jr.* Minneapolis: Fortress Press, 1992. A scholarly book on how King's life influenced the development of blacks and American culture.

Lerone Bennett Jr., *What Manner of Man: A Biography of Martin Luther King, Jr.* Chicago: Johnson, 1976. An insightful biography of King through his civil rights fights in 1964, with a postscript on his slaying in 1968.

Douglas Brinkley, *Rosa Parks*. New York: Penguin Putnam, 2000. A solid biography of the woman who helped ignite the Montgomery bus boycott.

Thomas R. Brooks, *Walls Come Tumbling Down: A History of the Civil Rights Movement 1940–1970*. Englewood Cliffs, NJ: Prentice-Hall, 1974. A comprehensive history of the fight for black rights in this period.

Michael Eric Dyson, *I May Not Get There with You: The True Martin Luther King, Jr.* New York: Free Press, 2000. While telling the story of King's fight for civil rights, this fine biography also explains how King's philosophy developed during his lifetime.

Adam Fairclough, *Martin Luther King, Jr.* Athens: University of Georgia Press, 1995. A solid, very insightful biography of King.

Marshall Frady, *Martin Luther King, Jr.* New York: Penguin, 2002. A fact-filled look at King's life.

Curt Gentry, *J. Edgar Hoover: The Man and the Secrets*. New York: W.W. Norton, 1991. The author explains how Hoover misused his power to attack King and other people he opposed.

Anthony Lewis, *Portrait of a Decade: The Second American Revolution*. New York: Random House, 1964. The book relies on *New York Times* stories to tell the early battle for civil rights.

David Levering Lewis, *King: A Biography*. Chicago: University of Illinois Press, 1978. One of the best biographers on King, Lewis offers a fascinating look at King's life.

Louis E. Lomax, *The Negro Revolt*. New York: Harper & Brothers, 1962. The author discusses the historical roots of the Civil Rights movement through King's early years as a leader.

Diane McWhorter, *Carry Me Home: Birmingham, Alabama, The Climactic Battle of the Civil Rights Revolution*. New York: Simon & Schuster, 2001. A personal look at the violent protests in Birmingham.

Stephen B. Oates, *The Trumpet Sound: The Life of Martin Luther King, Jr.* New York: Harper & Row, 1982.

Fred Powledge, *The Civil Rights Movement and the People Who Made It*. Boston: Little, Brown, 1990. Separate biographies of major black leaders in civil rights.

Diane Ravitch, ed., *The American Reader: Words That Moved a Nation*. New York: Harper Perennial, 1991. A collection of songs, speeches, and other written material that helps explain U.S. history.

Richard Reeves, *President Kennedy: Profile of Power*. New York: Simon & Schuster, 1993. One of the best biographies written on Kennedy.

Margaret Truman, *Harry S. Truman*. New York: William Morrow, 1973. Truman's daughter gives a solid portrayal of one of the nation's strongest presidents.

William L. Van Deburg, ed., *Modern Black Nationalism: From Marcus Garvey to Louis Farrakhan*. New York: New York University Press, 1997. Deburg uses their writings to explain the historical development of black leaders.

William Roger Witherspoon, *Martin Luther King: To The Mountaintop*. Garden City, NY: Doubleday, 1985. A solid biography of King that includes many wonderful pictures that help bring to life the civil rights leader and his era.

Internet Sources

Ronald L.F. Davis, "Creating Jim Crow." www.jimcrowhistory.org

John F. Kennedy, "Report to the American People on Civil Rights" (speech transcript), June 11, 1963, John Fitzgerald Kennedy Library. www.cs.umb.edu.

Martin Luther King Jr., "I Have A Dream" (speech transcript), August

28, 1965, Creighton University. www.creighton.edu.

Martin Luther King Jr., "Letter From A Birmingham Jail" (speech transcript), Creighton University. www.creighton.edu.

Martin Luther King Jr., "The Quest for Peace and Justice" (Nobel lecture transcript), December 11, 1964. www.nobel.se.

Martin Luther King Jr., "To The Mountaintop" (speech transcript), April 3, 1968, Creighton University. www.creigton.edu.

Websites

MLK Online (www.mlkonline.com). An Internet site dedicated to Martin Luther King Jr.

The Martin Luther King Jr. Paper Project (www.stanford.edu). A Stanford University Internet site on King.

The King Center (www.thekingcenter.com). The Internet site for the foundation Coretta Scott King established in 1968 to continue the legacy of Martin Luther King Jr.

INDEX

PICTURE CREDITS

About the Author

Michael V. Uschan has written nearly thirty books including *The Korean War*, for which he won the 2002 Council of Wisconsin Writers Juvenile Nonfiction Award. Mr. Uschan began his career as a writer and editor with United Press International, a wire service that provided stories to newspapers, radio, and television. Journalism is sometimes called "history in a hurry." Mr. Uschan considers writing history books a natural extension of skills he developed in his many years as a working journalist. He and his wife, Barbara, reside in the Milwaukee suburb of Franklin, Wisconsin.